MECHANICAL
COLOR SEPARATION SKILLS
FOR THE COMMERCIAL ARTIST

MECHANICAL
COLOR
SEPARATION
SKILLS
FOR THE COMMERCIAL ARTIST

TOM CARDAMONE

ILLUSTRATED BY THE AUTHOR

VNR **VAN NOSTRAND REINHOLD COMPANY**
New York   Cincinnati   Toronto   London   Melbourne

Copyright © 1980 by Litton Educational Publishing, Inc.
Library of Congress Catalog Card Number 78-25572

ISBN 0-442-21486-3
ISBN 0-442-21487-1 (pbk.)

Printed in the United States of America

Designed by Tom Cardamone and Ann Kahaner
Cover design by Ann Kahaner

Published by Van Nostrand Reinhold Company
A division of Litton Educational Publishing, Inc.
135 West 50th Street, New York, N.Y. 10020

Van Nostrand Reinhold Limited
1410 Birchmount Road, Scarborough, Ontario M1P 2E7, Canada

Van Nostrand Reinhold Australia Pty. Limited
17 Queen Street, Mitcham, Victoria 3132, Australia

Van Nostrand Reinhold Company Limited
Molly Millars Lane, Wokingham, Berkshire, England

16   15   14   13   12   11   10   9   8   7   6   5   4   3   2   1

Library of Congress Cataloging in Publication Data

Cardamone, Tom.
  Mechanical color separation skills.

  Includes index.
  1. Photoengraving.   2. Color separation.   I. Title.
TR97 .C35   686.2'327   7 -25572
ISBN 0-442-21486-3
ISBN 0-442-21487-1 pbk.

Table of Contents

To Ann

Introduction

This text deals directly with basic problems, situations, conditions and information necessary for the advertising artist, illustrator, designer or art director to function in a professional manner. It offers information to the beginning artist and assistant art director as well. It would take years of experience, not in one, but in a variety of agencies and studios (both large and small) to acquire the understanding of these basic, involved necessities.

In order to become a professional advertising artist, designer or art director, one must understand particular production requirements that directly affect the preparation of art and photography for reproduction. The professional advertising artist must know them because he prepares the work, and the art director must know them because they directly affect creation, ordering and direction of its preparation. Logically, the more a person knows about the available reproduction processes and material, the broader his scope for creative experimentation, and the better his opportunity for success in this highly competitive field.

The printing industry, through know-how, trial and error, patience and experience, is striving to stimulate more buying of its products through efficiency and economy of operation. Technological developments have been made in equipment through automation. The age of electronics has created new methods, resulting in new technical developments. So vast is the involvement of technical data in printing methods and graphic arts that to compile it would require many cumbersome volumes. For the individual to keep abreast of this rapid advancement on each level of all areas would be an Herculean achievement. Nevertheless, he must endeavor to absorb as much as possible if he hopes to be a professional advertising artist.

In view of the fact that there is so much going on around him, often reading of a new development in something or other, the advertising and graphic artist is somewhat under pressure. Should he slacken for a while, he may find himself far behind and many will pass him. This may sound rather severe and, in a sense, it is. To keep a wheel in motion, a source of energy is needed. Such is this text.

While the industry is constantly changing its complexion, it does not mean all that has gone before is no longer useful. On the contrary. It should be obvious that there exists the small, the medium and the large in all phases of advertising. Generally, "the new" is used by the "largest" while the "medium" endeavors to grasp what it can and the "small" experiences it in dribs and drabs — some may never have the opportunity to experience it at all.

With few exceptions no one can predict where he will work, where and how he will obtain his field experience, nor can he foresee his progress. Realize also that agencies and studios (large or small) do not operate in the same way. Therefore, what is required of one may not be so of another. The student (or beginner) reads and hears of the latest advertising production innovations and procedures in school . . . but he may never have the good fortune of being exposed to them in the field. It is on this premise that I offer a variety of problems and information (old and new) that the advertising artist must know and will encounter regardless of where he will work.

Despite the long training in graphic art and production schools, many young artists often find themselves wandering aimlessly from place to place looking for work. Tremendous confidence and self assurance is instilled in them in school. However, while this factor plays an important role in their development, it is not enough. This is, of course, primarily in reference to the average student. These men and women are our future agency production men, studio board men, every-day layout artists, illustrators, etc.

In essence, stress should be laid upon the importance of the psychological effect upon the graphic artist as a result of his first exposure to the reality of the advertising business.

After the glamour of art school, the contrasting disciplinary requirements of advertising procedure on a professional level sometimes confuse the beginner. He may lose confidence and a future illustrator may fall by the wayside. Or he may fall into some obscure corner of the advertising world, just existing . . . never finding the opportunity to further develop his dormant capabilities. Sadly enough, this happens to many of the ''gifted'' artists as well.

Familiarization is perhaps one-half the ability to do a job. That is the primary purpose of this text . . . to acquaint the reader with the terms and procedure needed to survive in the business; to impose an understanding of the meaning of quality and how it may be achieved; to conveniently record examples of what should or shouldn't be done in the buying or preparing of art work for advertising and in the final analysis, to act as a platform in support of his aspirations.

Chapter 1: Line Art

In **reproduction** the definition of the term "line art" (or "line copy") is often confusing. Let us start by first clarifying the definition of this expression. It does **not mean** "black and white," nor should the word "line" be literally interpreted. "Line art" is simply **solid coverage of color,** whether it be black, green, orange or any color desired. Its shape may be in the form of type, lettering, dots, thin lines, thick lines, large masses and shapes or any combination of these. The reason it is commonly referred to as "black and white" is because the original art is generally prepared in black and white for photographic reasons related to the process of plate making. It may be **printed,** however, in **any color** required.

REPRODUCING LINE ART

The processes of reproducing art can be looked upon by the novice as quite a mysterious thing. Someone asked an artist, when shown a reproduction in a magazine . . . "You mean to tell me that you have to draw that same picture for each magazine?" Of course, this is an extreme case. Nevertheless, it is an example of how confused the layman can be. Well then, if you don't draw it seven hundred twenty-eight thousand times, how does it finally get into all those magazines and newspapers?

Art for reproduction falls into two categories: "Line Art" and "Tone Art." In line art there is only one value of color with no lighter or darker gradation, whereas in tone art you can have the full range of values from white through black. This chapter will deal only with line art.

Consider, for a moment, the well-known "finger-print" procedure as a simile of line reproduction. The skin of the pad on the underside of your finger has a grain. When pressed to an ink pad, then pressed to paper, the image created by the grain containing the ink is transferred to the paper (reproduction). The reason is simply that only the raised surfaces of the grain of skin are coated with the ink.

In order to reproduce a "line" drawing, a facsimile of the art must be created on a printing **surface.** The material containing this printing surface is called a "plate." There are basically four printing processes, nonetheless the procedure required to prepare "plates" for printing in all processes is essentially the same — the photographic process. The different types of printing processes can be listed as Letterpress, Lithography, Silk Screen and Intaglio. Our primary interest in this text is with both the relief plate, or "photoengraving," which is used in the Letterpress method of printing; and with the planographic or offset plate, which is

FIG. 1

Raised surface (mirror image)

ENGRAVING (relief plate)

Ink roller

Ink only on raised surface

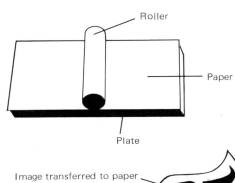

Roller

Paper

Plate

Image transferred to paper (Correct reading)

used in the Offset or Lithographic method of printing.

FIG. 1

Starting with the "relief" surface, which is essentially comparable to the fingerprint, the term, "photoengraving" comes into use. Actually, an "engraving," as it is commonly called, is a metal plate having a printing surface in raised portions in the **mirror image** of the image to be printed, so that when ink is applied to this surface and pressed to paper the image reads correctly. A rubber stamp is another example of relief printing. This **raised** surface containing the ink is termed "relief." Most original relief plates are "engravings." The process by which it is produced is called "Photoengraving." The printing process that uses engravings is called "letterpress."

For our purpose we will concentrate on understanding the **principle** and **essence** of this process rather than becoming too deeply involved in the mechanics.

FIG. 2

In the photoengraving process, line art (often referred to as "line copy") is photographed and a "line" film negative is made. This film is confined to black (opaque) and clear areas. All white areas in the original are opaque in this film; the line areas are clear.

The film negative is then stripped or taped onto a piece of clear acetate called a "flat." Then, a sheet of polished zinc, copper, or magnesium that has been made sensitive to light with a chemical solution and whirled to

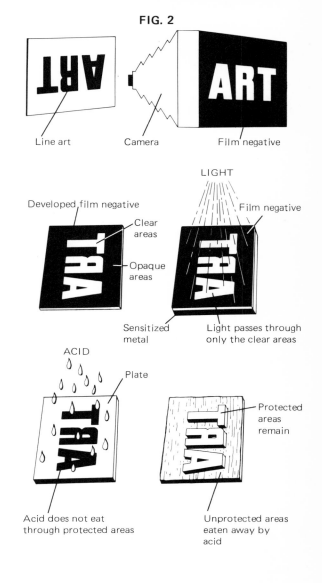

FIG. 2

Line art · Camera · Film negative

LIGHT

Developed film negative · Clear areas · Opaque areas · Sensitized metal

Film negative · Light passes through only the clear areas

ACID · Plate · Protected areas remain

Acid does not eat through protected areas · Unprotected areas eaten away by acid

THE LINE PLATE
(engraving)

dry evenly is placed under the flat in a vacuum frame and exposed to powerful lights. The clear areas in the film negative permit the passage of light. Those areas to the plate surface exposed to the light after developing become acid-resistant. The white areas of the original, being **opaque** on the photo negative, block out the light. Thus the chemical is washed away when the plate is developed. The developed plate is now ready for etching.

The plate is etched in a bath solution of nitric acid, which eats away the unprotected metal to the desired depth to make a satisfactory relief plate. The end result is a metal surface containing etched-out areas, leaving in raised portions an exact replica, in reverse position, of the original art. These raised portions, when covered with ink and pressed to paper, will leave an identical impression of the original art—similar to the common rubber stamp.

LITHOGRAPHY

Planographic or "Offset" Plate

FIG. 3

This thin, flat metal surface (zinc or aluminum) is chemically sensitized so that after a film negative has been photographically exposed to it and developed the image remains, in chemical form, on the surface of the metal.

Those portions of chemical on the metal surface that were exposed to light (the clear areas on the negative) will remain after developing and washing. The chemical surface on the metal that was not exposed to light (the black areas on the negative) will wash away exposing the bare metal surface.

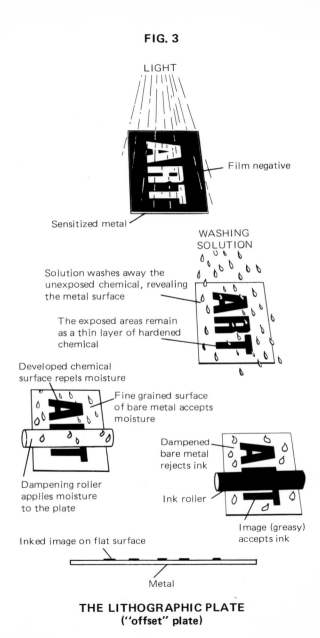

FIG. 3

LIGHT

Film negative

Sensitized metal

WASHING SOLUTION

Solution washes away the unexposed chemical, revealing the metal surface

The exposed areas remain as a thin layer of hardened chemical

Developed chemical surface repels moisture

Fine grained surface of bare metal accepts moisture

Dampened bare metal rejects ink

Dampening roller applies moisture to the plate

Ink roller

Image (greasy) accepts ink

Inked image on flat surface

Metal

THE LITHOGRAPHIC PLATE
("offset" plate)

This photosensitive chemical is essentially a grease-base substance which will repel moisture but accept a grease-base ink. The bare metal has a very finely grained surface which will accept moisture and repel the ink.

The Offset Lithography Press
FIG. 4

In Offset printing the plate does not transfer the image directly to the paper as in Letterpress, but to a rubber cylinder (blanket) that then "offsets" it onto the paper. Therefore, the image on the offset plate (lithographic plate) is not reversed—it is reversed when transferred to the blanket but reads correctly when offset onto the paper.

ART PREPARATION
FIG. 5

Your line art may be prepared using any technique, trick or device you desire and any size not more than six times larger or smaller than the reproduction size for best results. The important thing to remember is to keep the coverage of ink (or paint) **opaque** and black. When photographed, the camera will pick up nothing but the white shapes reflected from the original art and develop as black areas on film. The black (opaque) shapes will not be recorded; consequently these shapes do not develop on the negative emulsion and are washed away, leaving **clear** shapes on a **black** film. In other words the black images of the art act as a mask on the negative because they do not reflect the intensity of light required to fully expose the negative. Any sharp deviation in the consistency of coverage in the original

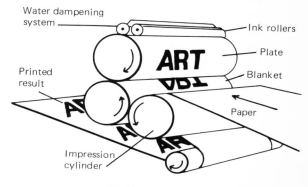

Water dampening system

Ink rollers

Plate

Blanket

Printed result

Paper

Impression cylinder

OFFSET PRESS

FIG. 5

Art must be clean, opaque and black, for good reproduction.

If art is weak or gray, it will reproduce poorly.

15

art will more than likely result in a breakup of the image on the negative.

REDUCTION
FIG. 6

With the exception of the point just mentioned, the reproduction of line art S/S (same size) is, in itself, generally not a problem. However, trouble begins when a reduction or enlargement is necessary. It is understandable that the inexperienced artist (or experienced for that matter) is sometimes so engrossed in his technique and style of line that he loses sight of the fact that his drawing is to be reproduced a different size . . . smaller, for example. What he doesn't realize (or at least may not take into consideration) is that while the **overall size** decreases, so does the **weight of the lines.** If the lines are too thin in the original, it may be impossible to hold them open on the negative and develop them clearly on the plate, resulting in broken lines when printed.

With experience, you will eventually develop an "eye" for proper thickness or weight of line in your drawing.

The word "copy" has two meanings. To the copywriter it means headlines or text matter. A printer or platemaker interpets its meaning to be "anything that is to be photographed for a printing plate." It is usually referred to as "copy for camera" or used in conjunction with a category of art work such as "line copy" or a "halftone copy." In essence, type as well as drawings, paintings, photographs, etc., can be referred to as art or copy — "art" being more specific, "copy" a general term.

FIG. 6

ORIGINAL ART

Poor reproduction (broken lines) when art is improperly prepared

Clean (sharp) reduction when art is correctly prepared

STRIPPING
FIG. 7

There are two means of reducing line copy for reproduction. Frequently the art is done larger, so that the mechanical, usually prepared reproduction size, might contain just the type and a light blue outline indicating the area to be occupied by the art.

The mechanical is then photographed by the platemaker as one unit and the original art is photographed separately, reducing it to the size indicated by the blue guide line on the mechanical.

Both film negatives (the line film negative of the type and line film negative of the art) are then pieced together following the blue outline on the mechanical for proper positioning. This is called a "strip-in." These combined films are then exposed to metal. This method usually produces the **truer** reproduction of the art because of its directness in preparation—art to photo negative, negative to plate.

If the type and the line drawing are reproduction size, all the elements can be pasted-up (in mechanical form) in their proper arrangement. The platemaker simply prepares one line film negative of the entire assembly. For more detailed information regarding mechanicals see the author's "Advertising Agency and Studio Skills."

FIG. 8

Another method of reducing line copy is to **photostat** it down to reproduction size. A photostat is a comparatively inexpensive photocopy. The difference between a photostat and a photograph is basically in the

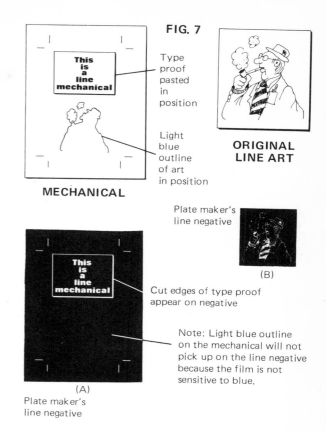

FIG. 7

Type proof pasted in position

Light blue outline of art in position

MECHANICAL

ORIGINAL LINE ART

Plate maker's line negative

(B)

Cut edges of type proof appear on negative

Note: Light blue outline on the mechanical will not pick up on the line negative because the film is not sensitive to blue.

(A)
Plate maker's line negative

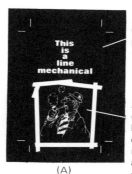

(A)

Cut edges painted out (opaqued)

Area to be occupied by line art cut out of negative and replaced with negative of art (B)

END RESULT

negative. A photographic negative is black and clear on transparent film—a photostatic negative is black and white on opaque **paper.**

Photostats are available in two general types—glossy (for line work) and matte (for tone work). While the quality of a photostat copy can hardly be compared with that of a photographic copy, it does play a very important role in production. A glossy photostat of line art can be used **as copy** for reproduction if it is **sharp and clean,** i.e., strong blacks and whites, whereas the inferior quality of the matte stat is a deterrent in its use as copy for camera.

FIG. 9

Photostating the art to size and cementing it into position on the mechanical along with the type make it possible for the platemaker to shoot the mechanical as a complete unit without having to strip in the art.

In addition to economy, stating the art to size and placing it into position on the mechanical offer an excellent visual of how it fits within the area before plating. Should it need to be made larger or smaller, it can easily be done by shooting another stat. Having reduced the art to the required reproduction size and placed it in position on the mechanical, it can be used as art for reproduction only if the **quality** of the stat measures up to your standards. Otherwise, it can be used in position on the mechanical as a **guide** for stripping by the platemaker.

The stat image will then be deleted from the film negative and replaced by a film negative photographed directly from the original. However using the photostat as copy for camera is

FIG. 8

PHOTOGRAPHIC FILM NEGATIVE

PHOTOSTAT PAPER NEGATIVE

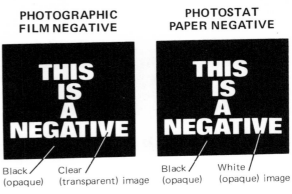

Black (opaque)   Clear (transparent) image

Black (opaque)   White (opaque) image

FIG. 9

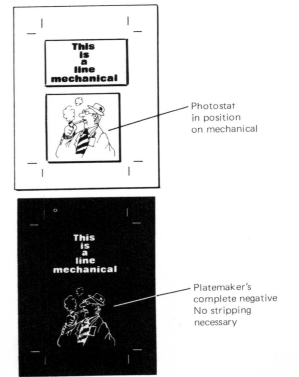

Photostat in position on mechanical

Platemaker's complete negative No stripping necessary

generally the easiest way to handle it.

While you must be concerned with the weight of line, you must also be aware of the negative space in reductions. The opening in letter formations such as A, B, P or the space between characters can "plug-up" (close-up) in extreme reductions. Art details that are too close or cross-hatching that is too dense could plug-up. Keep your art "open" in the detail or shadows and avoid ultrabold type faces when anticipating severe reductions.

FIG. 10

When art is copied, the copy is referred to as "a step removed" from the original. Both photographic and photostatic copies are two steps removed—the negative (first step) and the positive print (second step). Briefly, the quality of a photo copy is generally superior to that of a photostat copy. Nevertheless, with each step removed there is an expected loss of quality. Therefore, if you use a copy print (photographic or photostatic) as art in the mechanical, you are starting out two steps removed from the original. When the platemaker copies it for plating, his negative is a third step removed.

FIG. 11

If the platemaker shoots the line art **directly,** his negative is only **one** step from the original. He will make his plate from this negative. Consequently, he loses a **minimum** of the original's quality.

The reason for comparison is that there should be a time to use one and not the other when you are striving for excellence in reproduction. This, of course, will depend largely upon the nature of the art, the method of reproduction, the budget available and the nature of the job.

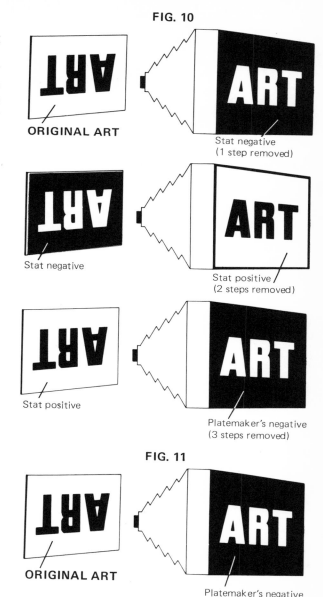

FIG. 10

ORIGINAL ART

Stat negative
(1 step removed)

Stat negative

Stat positive
(2 steps removed)

Stat positive

Platemaker's negative
(3 steps removed)

FIG. 11

ORIGINAL ART

Platemaker's negative
(1 step removed)

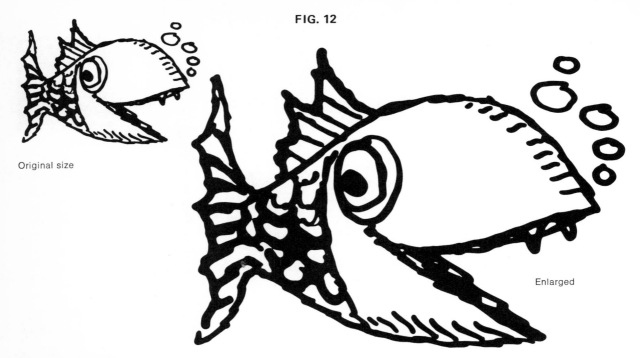

FIG. 12

Original size

Enlarged

ENLARGEMENTS

Making an enlargement (more commonly referred to as a "blow up") is a fairly common procedure. There are two significant considerations when working with enlargements. One is distortion. For example, a straight line of type may curve, or a symmetrical border could be twisted out of square. Anticipate this kind of problem. It could ruin a job. Once again — the photo copy will present less of a problem than a stat copy.

The second consideration is that the art or type may break up or become ragged when making extreme enlargements.

Because of these considerations, enlargements are rarely made directly from the original by the platemaker. Your best bet would be to have a photostat copy made on which you can "clean up" (retouch) broken lines or imperfections should they exist.

When "blackening" areas on a photostat negative you might try using black paint rather than ink. Paint doesn't stain as some inks do, so that if you must remove the black for some reason or another it will be cleaner.

One approach used to control the sharpness of an enlargement is to have the negative blown up larger than required (providing it doesn't reach prohibitive proportions), clean it where necessary, then have the positive reduced to the size you need. It will get sharper and cleaner in the reduction.

A word of caution — if you are working with machine-set or hand-set type, there is a chance that it will present a problem. Enlarging transfer type could be even more troublesome. You would be amazed at its apparent poor quality when enlarged —perhaps impossible to clean.

However, photo type should be able to withstand extreme enlargements with literally no noticeable roughness or break-up. Corners of sans serif type faces may lose their sharpness. If you use a felt-tip pen for finished line art, be certain it is a warm black or at least opaque. Some surfaces you draw on such as vellum or acetate have an effect on the opacity of the line. If the line is gray or watered down, usually bluish, it will reproduce poorly.

FIG. 12

Blow-ups present an interesting effect at times and can be utilized to your advantage. For example, you can do a line drawing in a stylized, loose line, smaller than required, and enlarge it. The line will break up and may produce an interesting effect. You might experiment with various lines on different paper.

In preparing line art you can use any medium you choose, providing it leaves a clean black opaque impression on the surface. "Clean" does not refer to the style of line but rather to its blackness. Charcoal, for example, does not necessarily produce smooth lines but leaves a clean black impression. The surface of the paper you use in conjunction with the medium you draw with will leave impressions according to the fineness or coarseness of its surface.

You must always be aware of your drawing as it will appear in reproduction. It is a matter of "feel," a sense of judgment which matures with the experience of seeing your work reproduced. Some artists may argue against this. They want nothing to interfere with their style or approach. After you have done many jobs and know your capabilities and the limitations of printing processes, perhaps you can be more independent. You will work hard enough in the initial execution of a drawing without having to take it back to heavy up the lines or open up the detail. This is all unnecessary work for you and annoying to the purchaser. Should this occur too often, it may impair your opportunity for future work. In addition to the business standpoint, don't lose sight of the fact that reproductions of your work can be used as samples. The artist who complains, "The original was much better" or ". . . What happened to it? My original was much more delicate (or stronger)," should realize that he will have to give some leeway to the available methods of reproducing his work and conform to their rules in order to attain the **best results.** The industry is diligently working for better quality . . . every day something new is rising to the surface.

It takes time.

Chapter 2: The Halftone Plate

CONTINUOUS TONE ART

Continuous tone art is composed of variations in values of black and/or color, such as a wash drawing, oil painting, photograph, transparency, etc. The changes of value may be sharp (postery), or subtly blended in a range from white through black (light to dark).

A painting intended to be hung on the wall of someone's living room for the admiration of its viewers can be prepared in any style, technique or medium suitable to the artist. At the time of its creation the artist is not concerned with screen, plates, paper stock, inks, budget, client's or printer's requirements. He usually paints to please himself.

However, painting for reproduction can be more complex. In the previous chapter on **line** reproduction you learned that when photographed, the original line art is transformed into a clear area on an opaque film. . . no gradations in the drawing will photograph.

FIG. 13

Should you photograph **tone art** for **line platemaking,** the results would be broken, mottled black and white shapes — i.e., any value in the original of 40%-50% intensity may not pick up at all or will barely appear as weak broken shapes, the lighter values will not register at all, and the darker values will fill in solid. Consequently, the end result would be an unfaithful reproduction of the original. Most printing is done with one shade or hue of ink. Changing the tonal value of the ink in order to recreate tone art has its limitations, although much research is being done along these lines. A successful method that best approaches **continuous-tone** printing, called Photogelatine, has been in use for a number of years but is presently extremely limited in its commercial use. The results of its efforts to service the industry's demands remain for the future to unfold.

Aside from aesthetic reasons the purpose of an advertising illustration is to create certain visual results. Just as line art production has its rules, though relatively simple, so does the production of tone art. So many things influence the end result in printing that countless hours can be spent in its study. Knowing the limitations of the available facilities will save hours of wasted effort and insure more pleasing results. **Suppose we look in on the complexities of production and study those aspects that mostly affect you as an artist, designer or art director.**

Due to the fact that operators involved in the various printing processes have numerous titles, it may be simpler, for the purpose of clarification, to refer to the person who photographs the art as the "cameraman," the person who works on the negatives for the plate as the "stripper," and the person who prepares the plate as the "platemaker" . . . regardless of process. For further simplification let us continue this discussion based on the offset lithographic method of printing.

If the value of ink does not change during printing to conform with the variations in value of the original, then perhaps the **illusion** of change can be achieved.

FIG. 14

During your studies in school you are invariably introduced to methods of creating value changes in **line drawings.** Among these methods you will find dry brush, cross-hatch and stipple. For a clearer understanding of the principle employed in printing tone art, study for a moment one of these methods — stipple, for example.

Note that the lighter tones are a comglomeration of small dots a certain distance apart. As your eye moves into the darker areas, observe that the dots increase in quantity and size, lessening the spaces around them. Finally, in the deeper and blacker areas, the dots are so close together and so numerous that they overlap, covering so much of the background that the area appears as a black shape with white dots diminishing into a solid mass of black. In this manner you create the optical illusion of tone effects using only **one value of ink.**

HALFTONE ENGRAVING

Until the 1880's art for reproduction had to

FIG. 13

Tone art shot for line plating
(poor results)

FIG. 14

STIPPLE DRAWING

be prepared using these line methods and had to be skillfully engraved by hand into wood cuts; this is almost a lost art today. Between 1880 and 1893 it was the genius of the pioneers Horgan, Glietsch, Ives, the Levys and Kurtz that made possible the process of tone reproduction used in the graphic arts today. This process is referred to as "Halftone Reproduction."

FIG. 15

This halftone printing plate is based on the same structure as the stipple drawing in that its surface contains dots and masses of varying sizes. The difference between the free-hand stipple drawing and the halftone printing plate is in the mechanical structure and uniformity of the dots. Let us examine the process of its preparation.

FIG. 15

HALFTONE REPRODUCTION

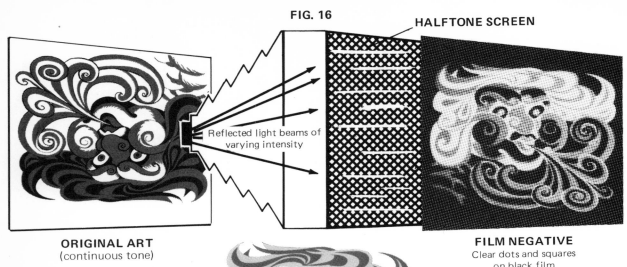

FIG. 16

HALFTONE SCREEN

ORIGINAL ART
(continuous tone)

Reflected light beams of varying intensity

FILM NEGATIVE
Clear dots and squares
on black film

HALFTONE REPRODUCTION

FIG. 16

A process similar to that used in the making of a **line** plate is followed, except that a ''screen'' must be used in the preparation of the photographic halftone negative. The halftone negative is made by inserting a ruled screen film between the camera lens and the sensitized film. This screen is made up of diagonal cross-hatched lines, varying from 55 to 300 lines per linear inch (a 55 screen, for example, contains 3,025 dots per square inch, etc.) In offset printing a standard 133 screen is generally used. Reflected light passing through the screen breaks down the original art into various sized clear dots and squares on the negative.

FIG. 17

In white and light areas on the **plate** the dots are smaller than in dark or black areas. That is, just as the values change from white to black, so does the **size** of the dots from small to large. Small dots in light areas progressively get larger until they merge into each other, creating the illusion of a white dot on black in

FIG. 17

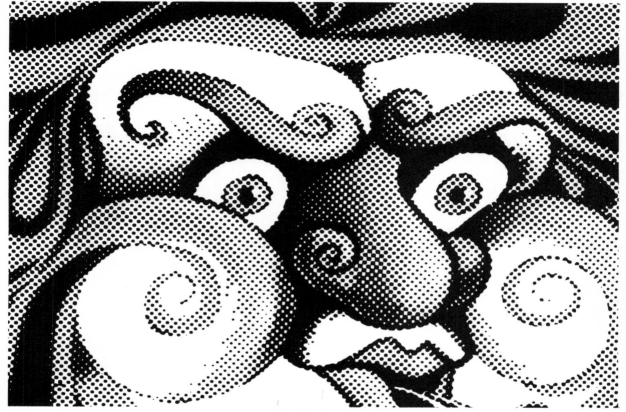

Magnification of
Halftone Reproduction
(black dots and squares)

the dark areas. However, the number of dots per square inch is the same.

For simple identification, an example of halftone printing can be found in any daily newspaper. Note, in viewing the picture at normal reading distance, that the dot formation (created by the screen) is unapparent. But upon closer examination, six inches from the page or through a magnifying glass, you will be amazed to find that what appears to be a continuous blend of tones is really a maze of minute black dots of various sizes. Thus, printing in only **one color of ink,** this screen creates the **optical illusion** of continuous-tone.

Chapter 3: Screen Tints

"Budget" is an important word in advertising. When a specific job is discussed and a particular method or approach is decided upon, an unsatisfactory artistic result is usually due to the budget. When it concerns only one job, it may be difficult to understand why a secondary method is employed to create certain results for the sake of economy. However, after several similar jobs by the end of the year, the saving (or spending) adds up to much more than just a few dollars. One of these economic measures is accomplished by using screening or shading sheets.

There is generally a sizable difference in cost between line and halftone plates; combining both can, of course, be more expensive. Very often "line" art may need "tone" for accent, balance or any of a number of reasons. If the tone shapes desired are not complicated or do not blend into different values as they do in continuous-tone art, shading sheets or halftone screening is used.

Before entering this area of study, establish these important facts in your mind:

In producing a "line plate" the image on the

Original

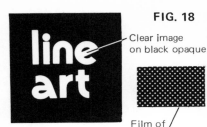

FIG. 18

Clear image
on black opaque

Film negative

Film of
uniform
clear dots (screen)

Film of dots
placed over
clear areas

A

END
RESULT

Original prepared in line only (without the tone).

Original prepared
with tone painted in.

B

C

Film negative

D

plate (which contains the ink) is created by a **clear** image on the film negative.

That image on the film negative is clear because the original art it was photographed from was solid black; the black did not photograph.

This image can be printed from the plate in any color ink you choose to apply to it.

The printed result will be a solid coverage of that color called "line." A film negative

containing all clear areas is called a "line negative."

The "halftone film negative" is not a completely clear image but one that is broken down into a dot formation because the original it was shot from contained tone variations and was photographed through a halftone screen.

Because this dot formation varies in size the effect it produces is one of changing values of

Film positive made from film negative. Black image on clear film.

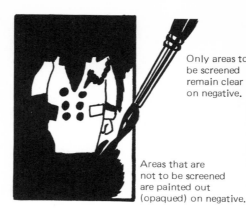

Only areas to be screened remain clear on negative.

Areas that are not to be screened are painted out (opaqued) on negative.

Negative film screen (clear dots on black).

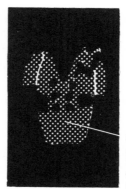

Screened film placed over ("stripped in") clear areas of opaqued negative.

E

PRINTED RESULT
After double exposure of film negative D and stripped assembly E

FIG. 18

the color ink applied to it.

A line negative and plate are generally less expensive than a halftone negative since they are less complicated to produce.

However, if a **tone effect** is desired in a **line** plate without the expense of preparing tone art and halftone plate, the screening method can be employed. This effect can be achieved in both the negative stage or in the plate making operation.

Suppose a negative film of uniformly sized and spaced **dots** is placed over the **clear** areas of a line film negative, as in Fig. 18A. It would develop on the plate as such and print an **even tone effect** of the color of ink that is applied to it — although the **ink color itself has not been changed.** This tone effect is called a "screened tint" or "benday."

For example, if Fig. 18B was rendered as such in the original art, i.e., a line drawing with **printed-in tone areas,** it would **have** to be photographed as a "facsimile" halftone; which means an exact reproduction of the art as it appears in the original. However, if only the line drawing was prepared in the original without the tone areas, Fig. 18C, it could then be shot in line and the tone areas stripped in by the film stripper, achieving the same desired effect at a lower cost.

Should the art require tone areas to be **modeled** or **changed in value,** then you would have to prepare the original with those areas painted and have a facsimile halftone plate made . . . in this case a screen tint would not serve the purpose. Although many unusual effects can be achieved with the screen or shading sheet technique, it is usually confined to an **overall even** tone effect.

Originally, this technique was exclusively employed by the platemaker or film stripper. All the artist had to prepare was the line drawing, leaving the desired tone areas blank or painting a light blue wash directly on the art in the desired tone areas (light blue is not picked up by the negative). The film stripper or platemaker would then strip in or double print the specified pattern or tone in those areas either on the negative or directly to the plate during the process of its preparation. There are innumerable patterns in positive and negative form available in various screens and unusual configurations.

You simply indicate on the tissue over the art or in the margin the percentage or code number of the tone value you desire to have stripped into a particular area. Printers and platemakers have available charts from which you can make

FIG. 19

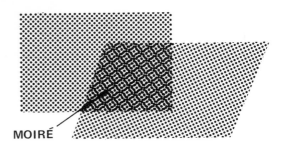

MOIRÉ

your selection. Combinations of one superimposed over the other create a moiré-pattern, which can be objectionable or present interesting values and textures that may add to your design. Stock screens are available in 9 values from 10%—90%.

FIG. 19

Stripping two or more screens together (butting or kissing), such as 40% with 60%, requires, care and a perfect alignment, because of the difference in the size of the dots. It might produce a moiré along the butting edge, an irregular heavy line between the two values, or an irregular white gap, sometimes called a "leak." The same holds true of butting a screen background against a silhouette halftone. Caution the platemaker to avoid these undesirable effects.

ORIGINAL

Adhesive-backed
shading sheet

FIG. 20

Place shading sheet
over area to be shaded

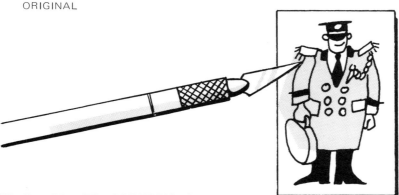

Cut and peel away

SELF-APPLIED SCREENS OR TEXTURE EFFECTS

When the term "benday" was used in the specification of a job, it was generally understood that the film stripper or platemaker would handle that phase of the operation. It was up to the discretion of the artist to choose the correct tone or texture best suited to the job. However, the availability of adhesive-back shading sheets later made it possible for the artist to strip in and control his own tone effects directly on the art.

FIG. 20

Because it is easily applied or removed, it offers the artist an immediate visualization of the effect he is seeking; whereas, if the screen or shading design was applied by the platemaker, the end result would largely depend upon the experience and craftsmanship of the platemaker and would not be seen until the job is proof printed (or a blue print made from the negative prior to plate preparation). Once the plate has been made, there is little that can be done to change it.

When these shading sheets were made available to the artist, they were referred to by their

trade name or as "shading sheets." If an art director or production manager instructed the artist to "put in such and such a sheet," he knew that the tint effects were not being stripped in by the platemaker (this was obvious). But today, the term "benday" is loosely used and often creates unnecessary confusion.

Various gelatin screens and stipple shading gelatins were invented by Benjamin Day in 1919. It was basically a mechanical means of economically achieving **even tone** or texture effects without making a "halftone" screen or plate. This was achieved through the application of various dot or linear patterns on the platemaker's negative or printed by transfer process directly on the plate.

It seems that now the commercially produced sheets are seldom referred to by their trade name but are called "benday". Therefore, during the instructions for a job, if the artist is told that a benday is to go here or there, he may very likely misinterpret the instructions to mean that it is going to be stripped in by the platemaker and prepare his art accordingly . . . or assume the opposite and strip in his own tones; in either case he may have done the wrong thing.

Now, you may ask," . . . what difference does it make who does it? . . ." To some there seems to be no difference. To those who regard their work as a serious endeavor, quality is also an important factor. The difference lies within the craftsmanship of the platemaker as compared with that of the artist and available material. If you feel confident that the platemaker will give you precisely what you want, that should he have to use his own judgment,

he will do a professional job, this is perhaps the best method to use. The end result also has to do with your ability to convey what you want.

Should the nature of the design be such that you must experiment a bit with it before you produce what you have in mind, then it might be better to apply your own tone . . . if you want to make a change, you can do so with relatively little effort.

In spite of this advantage, shading sheets can be deceiving in that when printed, the effect is often lighter or darker than it appeared in the original. Or the pattern often doesn't pick up cleanly when photographed. There are poor as well as quality grades of these sheets. While it may not be apparent to the naked eye, it is obvious when viewed through a magnifying glass that the impressions are not clean. The platemaker's camera is quite literal in what it sees and will not compensate for any imperfections in the art, unless it is observed by the photographer, who may be able to offer a little control. In addition to this, the sheen of some acetate shading sheets **may** interfere with the photography.

Once again, you have an example of a second step removed from the original. The **self-applied sheet** is already a printed formation which must be photographed with extra care in order to pick up its minuteness; the screen of shading designs **applied by the film stripper** is executed in the negative stage, which is much more direct.

In the long run, if you have worked with both methods, the chances are that you will prefer the "bendays" (screens) to be stripped in for you. The quality seems to be superior when working with a competent platemaker. On low budget jobs, where these tone effects might be used as a secondary accent or in small, insignificant areas, perhaps it might be economically feasible to apply the tones yourself; but should the tone play an important role in the design, the relatively small added cost of a strip-in should be disregarded.

Nevertheless, these sheets are here to stay and do help in many ways. Here are a few points to consider when using commercial shading sheets.

Purchase a good grade. The difference in cost (which is little) will be superseded by the production of a better product. Check the image printed on these sheets. Some will scrape away from the surface. Try scratching the surface lightly with your fingernail; if the pattern easily scrapes away, it may interfere with the quality. This type of sheet has its particular advantage; experiment with it. If your design calls for an effect that would require scratching away the pattern, you can do so with a razor blade or white paint mixed with "non-crawl."

Upon examining the texture through a magnifying glass, you will find the inferior brands have gray or broken impressions which are not apparent to the eye at normal reading distance, but do affect the quality of reproduction.

When cutting, use a new razor or freshly sharpened X-acto knife. Most art stores sell a special cutting stylus for their sheets. A light pressure is all that is required to cut through the surface.

When cutting along an area that is outlined in the drawing, cut in on the line rather than along its edge to ensure proper overlapping of the texture. This overlap, or "trap," will prevent little gaps along the edges and effect a cleaner butting of the tone.

After you have cut and burnished the sheet in position, clean it by **lightly** rubbing the surface with a piece of soft tissue **dampened** with thinner. Dampened, not saturated. Too much thinner will dissolve the wax-like adhesive behind the sheet and cause it to slide out of position.

If you want to lift a piece after it has been burnished, saturate it with thinner, and lift it carefully with the corner of a razor. After it has been lifted, you will find that a waxy deposit is left in its place. Do not attempt to draw over this wax. Clean it as well as possible first. Most erasers will only smear and streak the surface. Scrape it gently with the edge of a razor, holding the full edge flat against the surface. Then rub it down with tissue and thinner. Be sure that it is dry and clean before drawing over it.
area.

Shading sheets are also used to create surprints with type or drawings. Surprinting is the superimposing of solid color over tone of the same color (see page 40). An important thing to be careful of are the "cut" lines and edges of paper under the sheets as well as marks or wrinkles. They will show up as black lines in the reproduction.

For example, suppose you had to place a tone sheet over a line of type that does not have sufficient space around it. You can't just cut it out, cement it onto a larger piece of paper and place the shading sheet over it; the cut edges will show through.

FIG. 21

The thing to do here is to cement it onto a sheet of white paper large enough to accommodate the area to be converted into tone, then have a glossy negative stat made and black out the cut lines on that negative. Have the positive made and place your tone film onto this.

Some artists feel this is too much trouble. What they do is cut the type out, cement it onto a larger sheet of white paper and paint out the cut lines with white paint before placing the shading sheet over it. This is very deceiving and too often shows up in the repro as a faded out or broken area. White paint under the tone sheet can be used on small things such as a spot on the paper. Actually, the difference in whiteness of the paper and the white paint affects the reflection of the white paper between the texture, thus interfering with the intensity of the image when photographed.

There is one thing that should stand out among all others and that is the question of screen. Each printing process in conjunction with the stock (paper) used in printing requires a different-sized screen. For example, 65 screen is used for most newspaper printing, 120 screen for coated stock, and 133 screen for offset stock. A job can be held up or ruined because the wrong screen was used. While these films come in a variety of textures and tone values, they also are composed of so many dots or shapes to the linear inch (the same as in halftone screens). Be

FIG. 21

Desired tone area

Cut edge of type proof

Cut edge reproduces and shows through screen

STAT NEGATIVE
Black out cut marks

STAT POSITIVE
No cut marks

END RESULT

certain that you check this before selecting the sheet you need. For example, the particular value you choose may be composed of a 100 screen; if you are to use it in a newspaper ad... the result will be a blotchy broken mess.

Line and dot patterns are usually keyed in the margin according to screen size, such as "60 lines/inch," "23.50 lines/cm," "85 line," etc. However, the texture sheets may be keyed by a code number rather than screen size. By and large these textures are coarse and usually will not create reproduction problems.

It is advisable to avoid using these textures and patterns on art that is to be reduced in reproduction. For example, an 80 line screen when reduced 50% will become a 160 line screen — this could cause you headaches. If you must reduce the art, be sure to use the coarser textures or at least consult your production manager or printer.

You, the artist or designer, are creating certain visual effects. The more extensively you develop your sense of judgment in the use of these methods, the more sensitive you will become to the results.

In addition to shading sheets there are drawing papers available that are particularly effective in producing tones. One, called "Coquille Bristol," is conducive to pencil or crayon drawings.

Another is called "Duo-shade" board. It is a white drawing board, the surface of which contains an invisible texture of lines or dots. The texture is made visible (black) by the use of a chemical developer. It is available in one or two patterns of both light and dark values. To use it, simply pencil your drawing and ink it with pen or brush as you would on any surface. Be sure to use a good waterproof ink.

Then with a clean watercolor brush apply the developer to the area where you want the tone or texture. The pattern instantly appears. There is nothing difficult about the procedure; instructions are supplied with the board.

However, care should be taken during the penciling, as the graphite or unerased pencil lines may obliterate the pattern. Many artists do their initial penciling with a "non-reproducing" light blue. Because the blue does not reproduce, it eliminates the need to erase the drawing after it has been inked. The same could be used on the Coquille Bristol.

An example of this type of art preparation can be found in the comic sections of most newspapers. It is worth experimentation.

SURPRINT

DROPOUT

REVERSE

Chapter 4: Surprint/Dropout/Reverse

Selecting the proper type face and size plays an important role in the design of an effective ad. Needless to say, it requires training and experience to develop a sense of good judgment and understanding of both the psychological effect and aesthetic function of type design. Rather than delve into the fundamentals of type design in this volume, it may be best to remind the reader that there are many excellent books available on the subject. Nevertheless, there is one aspect of selecting type that unavoidably must be discussed here: "sur-print," "dropout," and "reverse."

SURPRINT

An element of design frequently employed is the use of surprint. Surprint is a solid color shape (such as type or a line drawing) superimposed over a halftone or screen of the **same color.** To achieve a surprint, a double exposure of two films (line and half-tone or line and screen) onto one plate, is used . . . producing the effect in one print-ing. Don't confuse it with anything else.

FIG. 22

It is **not** solid color superimposed over a **different** color (for all intents and purposes this might be called "overprinting"). To repeat, surprint is the superimposed combination of **line** and **tone** of the **same color,** i.e., black on gray (screen or HT), solid red on light red (screen or HT), solid blue on light blue (screen or HT), etc.

FIG. 23

Selecting the proper typeface and position for a surprint warrants careful consideration by the art director. All too often proofs come in with surprint type so broken and "chewed" by the dot formation (screen) of the halftone or screened tint that they are impossible to read (Fig. 23 A).

What is actually taking place? The enlargement (Fig. 23 B) reveals the screen dots to be heavier or as heavy as the type. . . thus interfering with its legibility. However, in Fig. 23 C a slightly heavier type face was used and positioned in a lighter area. Note in the enlargement (Fig. 23 D) the smaller dot formation does not break up the type as much.

In conclusion, the coarseness of screen, the tone value, as well as the paper surface should be considered in determining the face and size of type to surprint or drop out. Generally speaking, the finer screens do not present too great a problem. The danger lies in the coarser screens — 50 to 65, as used in newspaper reproduction—and in some cases 85 to 100, as used on machine finish papers.

FIG. 22

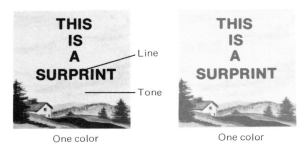

One color   One color

Two colors

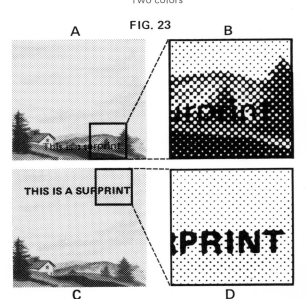

FIG. 23

DROPOUT

Students, as well as experienced artists, needlessly confuse the terms "dropout" and "reverse." Is there a difference? They both seem to imply the same effect.

"Dropout" is obviously the opposite of surprint in that during the process of preparing the plate the "line" shape (type or drawing) is **deleted** from the halftone or screen film negative of any one color or combination or colors.

You are aware of the composition of the dot formation in a halftone or screened plate. In order to give the **effect** of white type within this area, a photographic line film must be made of the type (black type on a clear background) and placed in position over the halftone film.

FIG. 24

During the process of platemaking, the film containing the black type acts as a mask, blocking out the light in those areas, preventing development of a dot formation within its shape; such as a stencil letter might do if you were to spray paint over it . . . only the area around it would accept the paint. The result is a halftone plate containing areas void of dots. Thus, when printed onto white paper, the effect is of white type on tone. Should the same plate be printed on a colored stock, say, blue, the **effect** would be blue type on tone. Either case is considered a "dropout," because of the absence of dots within the tone area, which is the result of a "mechanical" deletion (sometimes called "knock-out") of the tone dot. This applies to the dropping out of type, line drawings, or any **"line" shape.**

FIG. 24

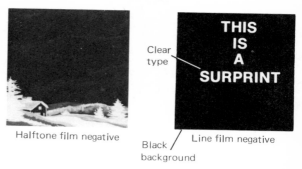

Halftone film negative

Clear type

Black background

Line film negative

SURPRINT

The HT film negative is exposed to the plate and removed and the line film negative is double exposed in position to create a surprint.

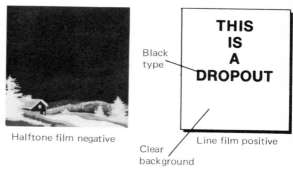

Halftone film negative

Black type

Clear background

Line film positive

DROPOUT

One film is placed over the other and both exposed simultaneously to create a dropout.

41

FIG. 25

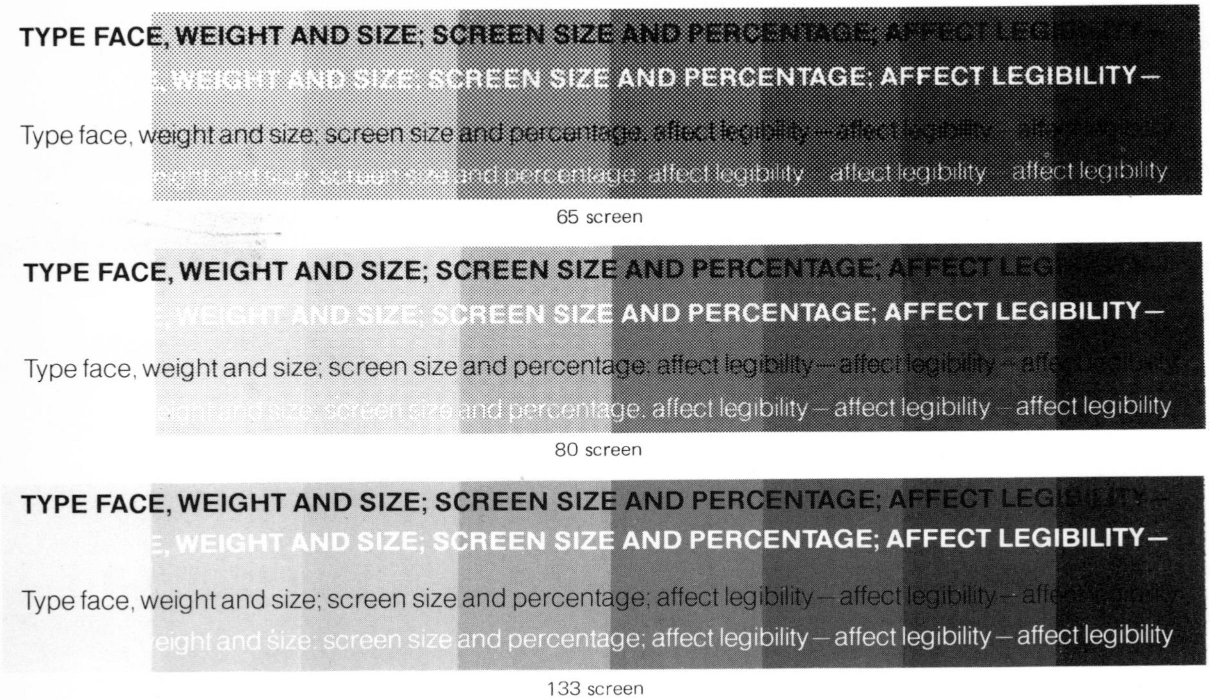

TYPE FACE, WEIGHT AND SIZE; SCREEN SIZE AND PERCENTAGE; AFFECT LEGIBILITY—

Type face, weight and size; screen size and percentage; affect legibility—affect legibility—affect legibility

affect legibility—affect legibility

65 screen

TYPE FACE, WEIGHT AND SIZE; SCREEN SIZE AND PERCENTAGE; AFFECT LEGIBILITY—

Type face, weight and size; screen size and percentage; affect legibility—affect legibility—affect legibility

80 screen

TYPE FACE, WEIGHT AND SIZE; SCREEN SIZE AND PERCENTAGE; AFFECT LEGIBILITY—

Type face, weight and size; screen size and percentage; affect legibility—affect legibility—affect legibility

133 screen

FIG. 25

While in a dropout (as in a surprint) the screen has a similar effect on the weight of the spaces dropped out, it transposes itself in that readability is better in the darker values than in the lighter.

FIG. 26
REVERSE

"Reverse" does **not** mean "facing the opposite direction," as in Fig. 26B. The proper term used to effect the "opposite direction" is called "flop," i.e., Fig. 26B is a "flop" of Fig. 26A.

"Reverse" refers to the **absense** of color within a **solid** color area of line (Fig. 26C).

The effect of white on a solid color is actually **part of the shape** of that color. It isn't a matter of deleting something from the film; there is no dot formation. The process of reversing the copy is accomplished by contacting the negative made of the original line drawing or type and making a positive, called **reversing** the film.

For example, the desired effect is white type

on a one color background. The original type is pasted onto white paper and the shape of the color background is outlined in red, directly on the paste-up (as in Fig. 26D). This red line is referred to as a "keyline" (see page 60).

A **film negative** is shot and a **film positive** is made from it (Figs. 26 E & F). The positive film contains **black type** and a **black keyline** on a **clear background.** The area outside the keyline is then opaqued by the film stripper (Fig. 26G). Now, when this film is exposed to a plate, the printed result would be white type on a colored background (Fig. 26H). Here we started out with black type on a white background in the original, but by making a film positive from the film negative, the platemaker obtains a "reverse" or "opposite" image (not "flopped").

This is one approach. However, should the original be prepared in white on a black shape (as in Fig. 26C), the first film shot from this, being the negative, would be a black line on a clear shape (as in Fig. 26G). The plate can then be made directly from this negative, thus eliminating three steps (Figs. 26 E, F & G) in the processing.

In essence, then, "dropout" generally refers to halftone or screens; "reverse" (or "opposite") is used in reference to solid color (line).

PROFESSIONAL APPROACH

The coarseness or fineness of screen in halftone reproduction determines, to a great degree, the approach in the preparation of art and photography. If the illustrator would seriously consider these facts while rendering, reproduc-

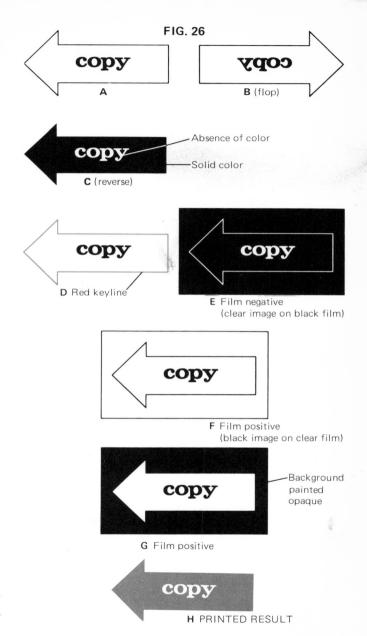

FIG. 26

A

B (flop)

C (reverse)
— Absence of color
— Solid color

D Red keyline

E Film negative (clear image on black film)

F Film positive (black image on clear film)

G Film positive
— Background painted opaque

H PRINTED RESULT

tion results would be much more satisfactory. So many illustrators and board artists complain that the reproduction of their art is unfaithful to the original. More than likely, this is true, but the fault may not be so much in the method of reproduction as it is in the art itself.

Your wrist watch may be inscribed "shock resistant". You take it for granted that the statement is true to a limited degree. As a test, you may slap it against your hand, or if you are daring enough, you might drop it from your waist to the floor, then check to see if it is still running. Chances are it will still be in good condition, depending upon the quality of its construction. Now, you certainly would not toss it from the roof of a building and expect to recover it intact.

In a broad sense, this is what some inexperienced art directors and illustrators do. They prepare art, shoot a photograph or order type disregarding the limitations of the reproduction process or the quality of the platemaker. Then after it has been reproduced and the proof compared with the original, they are disappointed with the results and complain. "This repro is terrible" or "Look at the original art — it's beautiful," or "Look at the subtle value changes in the art . . . they aren't in the repro . . ." They are throwing the watch from a rooftop, expecting to recover it in its original state.

There must be a way to honestly attempt to solve this unnecessary yet common problem. To begin with, the purpose of this book is not to defend platemakers, printers, or production people or to restrict illustrators, designers and art directors, but to establish a much needed understanding of each other's position — to point out, without prejudice, the existing working conditions for both sides.

Suppose an art director designed a layout for a newspaper ad that included halftone art (in addition to other line elements). At the very beginning of operations the art director should sit in with his production manager and discuss reproduction of the ad. After all, production is one job, art directing is another, but they often overlap. The art director is not expected to know **as much** about production as the production man nor the production man as much about art directing, nevertheless, one hinges on the other to a good degree, so why not accept each other's repsonsibility for what it is and establish cooperation and close liaison between each other?

Before type is set . . . before the artist or photographer is called in . . . the time to consult your production manager is in the planning stage. Together you will look for unforeseen snags according to the specifications of the publication. Search for repro problems that may affect the preparation of the art. Check type faces . . . perhaps the face chosen is too delicate to surprint or drop out of a halftone. Formulate the requirements, point out the restrictions . . . in general, go over it with a fine-tooth comb and you will be guaranteed better results. That's it! With this preliminary coverage employing production ingenuity economies can be effected through specifications. The art director can properly direct the execution of the art and mechanical in anticipation of pleasing results.

What does all this mean? Does it mean that the production manager has the last word in everything or that the art director can't make a move without his consent? Of course not! It simply means that as time goes on he can anticipate certain problems in the **designing stage** . . . he'll know what to avoid . . . he'll know the boundaries and design with an understanding of reproduction . . . the more he asks in the beginning, the less he will have to ask in the future. As a matter of fact, the important thing is that he will **know** when **to** and when **not to** consult his production manager.

So much for the art director and production manager. What about the illustrator? A competent illustrator will follow instructions. After all, he is going to produce the job according to specifications, and if he "goofs," his acquisition of future work will be limited. It is well known that asking questions is a way to learn. What is wrong with asking the art director what he means when an unfamiliar technical phrase is used in his instructions? Does it make sense to be proud, nod your head in acknowledgment (yet not know what he means), then prepare the art according to your own interpretation of something technical . . . at the risk of having it rejected? This should not have anything to do with "professional prestige." It is a working condition. It is inconceivable that we should be expected to know one another's jobs equally as well, but we should at least have an understanding of them because they all affect each other in some way during the overall procedure. While it may give you self-satisfaction to say . . . "I'm an artist! You're stifling my

talent . . ." it is less pleasant to hear ". . . I like your work from an artistic point of view but we can't use it because it reproduces poorly. We're **selling with the reproduction . . . not the original!"**

The original art is simply a means to an end.

PROCESS COLOR SEPARATION

Chapter 5: Process Color Separation

FOUR-COLOR PROCESS

Rather than expound the controversial theories on the **use** of color, the purpose of this section is simply to expose the importance of understanding color separation and the seriousness with which it should be regarded. The use of color, which actually has a great deal to do with individual taste, is unquestionably taught with much success in the better art schools and in many good books.

It might be broadly stated that there is no one way to do anything. Each job, each art department, each process, and each print shop has its own set of rules and specifications. Theoretically they are the same but their work procedure may vary.

Suppose we briefly discuss the **principles** of the **four-color process** of reproduction. The three primary process colors are yellow, magenta and cyan (yellow, red and blue); and by mixing them in various proportions, innumerable colors can be obtained.

Let us use a full color painting as an example. The process of mixing paints on your palette and applying them to paper is relatively straight forward, but **recreating** the finished painting by means of a printing plate is much more

FIG. 27

FOUR COLOR PROCESS SEPARATION

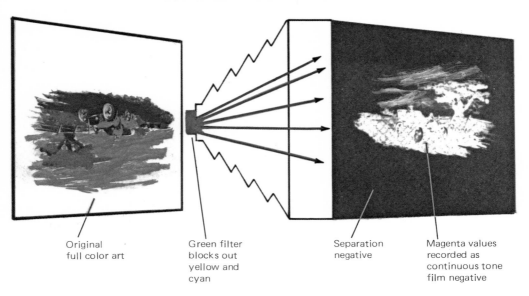

Original
full color art

Green filter
blocks out
yellow and
cyan

Separation
negative

Magenta values
recorded as
continuous tone
film negative

complex. The combination of colors is not printed in **one** impression from a **single** plate. In itself, it contains varying degrees of yellow, magenta, cyan and black. Due to the fact that only **one impression of one color is printed in a particular area at a time, regardless of the speed with which it is printed, a separate printing plate of each color must be made.** Therefore, to produce this full color effect, the original painting must be photographically dissected into the three primary colors, producing **separate film negatives.**

FIG. 27

The separator must analyze it for yellow, magenta and cyan content, then isolate each color by the use of filtration. To photograph the magenta in a subject, a green filter is used. It blocks out its components, yellow and cyan, permitting only the magenta to be photographed. To capture the cyan values in the original, an orange filter is used; its components, magenta and yellow, permit only the cyan to be photographed. To separate the yellow values a filter containing the other two colors, cyan and magenta, is used; this violet

FIG. 28

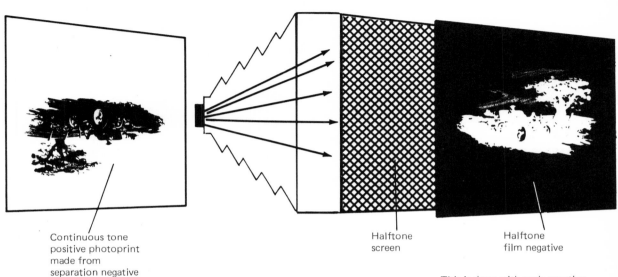

Continuous tone
positive photoprint
made from
separation negative

Halftone
screen

Halftone
film negative

This is done with each negative,
producing four separate halftone
negatives from which plates are made

filter will allow only the yellow to be photographed.

Although we have been thinking in terms of
three colors, it is well to remember that the
four-color process really involves the three
primary colors plus black. Black is used to
add strength to the detail and neutral shades
of grays, which are difficult to obtain with
the three primaries. In order to produce
a black negative, the original is shot through
one, two or the three preceding filters, with
exposure modified to suit the purpose.

FIG. 28

These **process separation negatives** are continuous tone (no dot formation) recordings of
the values of each color, but they cannot be
used for platemaking. They must be converted into **halftone** negatives.

One method of conversion would be first to
make a positive photoprint from the negative,
then to rephotograph the positive through a
halftone screen — thus producing a halftone
negative. This is done with all four negatives.

The direct method of color separation can

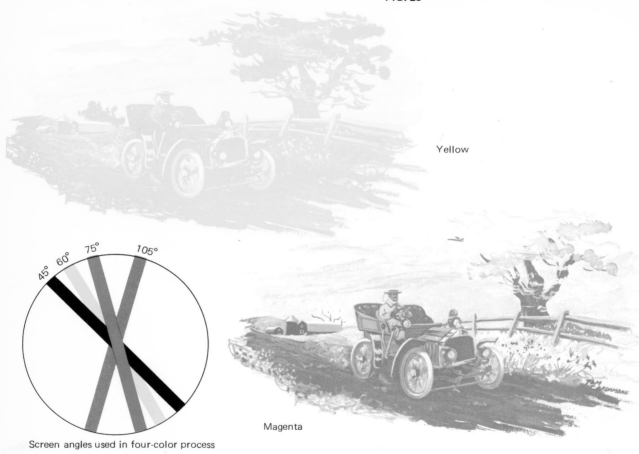

FIG. 29

Yellow

Magenta

Screen angles used in four-color process

also be employed; namely, to separate the colors through filtration and produce a halftone negative all in one operation. However, this is not common practice. The nature of the art and degree of correction required determine the choice of the photographic procedure to be used. These negatives are then used to prepare four separate plates.

If all these halftone plates had the same screen **angle** and each was printed over the order the halftone dots in each plate would cancel each other out. The printed result will appear as a blotchy, **uncontrolled** moiré pattern of dark and light squares, preventing

Cyan

Black

proper gradation of colors. To better understand moiré, take two shading sheets (see page 32) and place one over the other. Note the tiny symmetrical shapes and designs that form.

FIG. 29

In order to avoid an uncontrolled moiré pattern, each halftone film must be made at a different angle to control the placement of dots. The three color halftone negatives are made at a thirty degree deviation from each other; the yellow halftone negative is fifteen degrees between the red and black negatives. The screen size for the yellow plate is often changed to afford further color control.

FIG. 30

Yellow and Magenta

Yellow, Magenta and Cyan

Yellow, Magenta, Cyan and Black

Note Controlled Moire Pattern.

FIG. 30

Each of these color plates is printed individually, in register, one over the other. The order in which colors are printed depends upon the particular job and the discretion of the printer. Usually the yellow is printed first, followed by magenta, cyan and black.

This juxtaposition and minuteness of dots produces the **optical illusion** of full color **continuous tone.** It is all done with dots . . . think for a moment how many dots there would be in a **square inch** area printed in four

colors using a 150 screen . . . 90,000 dots. A simple 8 x 10″ area would contain approximately 7,200,000 dots! Incredible?

It should be realized that as yet no dyes have been discovered that will make perfect color filters, and photographic plates are not completely sensitive to all colors. Therefore, color separations are not exact. The degree of faithfulness to the original depends upon many things. The quality of the art is perhaps one of the most important. If the art contains poor, muddy colors, you can be sure that the reproduction is not going to be any better, perhaps worse. Each platemaker has his own technique in accord with the quality of his equipment and the technology he applies.

In addition to mechanical skill and artistic technique, color technicians require an intense knowledge of color composition, which consumes most of the time required to produce good color plates.

Because of the time and expense involved in actual platemaking and/or printing, preliminary steps· are taken to check quality. One relatively inexpensive method is to prepare color cells from the separation negatives before making plates.

These cells are called "Color-Keys" and consist of four separate colored halftones magenta, cyan, yellow and black) on a clear cell. Each, when superimposed one over the other, blends with it, creating a full-color image.

While this is an excellent method of checking before platemaking, you should realize that the grayness of each cell (although transparent) dulls the color. You must actually learn to read or interpret these Color-Keys. This can only come from experience in comparing the keys with the final reproduction.

Another method involves the "Transfer-Key," which is an actual printed four-color proof. The proof is made using a polyster sheet coated with a thin layer of light-sensitive ink pigment for each of the four colors. Each sheet is individually exposed to its respective halftone separation negative and transferred to a base material, removing the nonimage area. When printed and laminated in registration one over the other, a four-color proof is achieved.

Of course, the most accurate method of all is to make plates and run off pre-press proofs on a separate proofing press.

This set of proofs is known as "progs" (progressive proofs) and is sent to the art director or production manager for approval. Often it is printed in progressive combinations . . . a separate proof for each color plate or combination . . . magenta; yellow; cyan; black; magenta and yellow; magenta; yellow and cyan; magenta, yellow, cyan and black. This permits scrutiny of each color plate and mixture, which enables the art director or production manager to point out specific areas of each plate that may have to be corrected

An artist, while painting, has the advantage of being able to observe the effects of his mixture as he paints and perhaps to add or take out a little of one color or another. The color technician does not have this opportunity. He must use his knowledge and skill in preparing such plates, and it is not until all four colors are combined on one proof that he can see the results of his judgment. Sometimes a subject is corrected and proved three or four times, making corrections on the plates and in color control, before a satisfactory reproduction is obtained. Needless to say, it is a very complex undertaking and quite expensive.

Each platemaking process is dependent upon photography. The type of plate and reproduction principles involved vary with each printing method. The reason for these basic differences in procedure, both technical and mechanical, is due to the variety of reproduction problems. To add to the complexity, the paper stock used in printing also is a major factor in the measure of quality, fidelity, readability, etc., of the printed result. Because of these factors, best results are obtained in full color reproduction when the art director and production manager consult their platemaker and printer and study the job before going into production.

Full color photographic originals for reproduction fall into approximately four classifications.

The transparency: a full color photographic film positive. Also referred to as a "slide" or a "chrome."

The dye transfer: a full color print made from a transparency. While it appears to be a color photograph, it is actually printed in continuous tone with color dyes.

The C print: a full color photograph print made from a negative transparency (referred to as an "inter neg").

The Cibachrome: a full color photographic print also made from a transparency.

Each of these generally offers three levels of quality in prints: layout print, presentation print and reproduction (repro print). The price, of course, varies with each type. Which of these methods offers the best repro quality is debatable and dependent upon the job requirements. To a great degree the physical properties of each affects the retouching possibilities.

Another print (the least expensive of all) is the color stat. Because of its poor quality it is used in the preparation of dummies and layouts and to indicate position on mechanicals. It is rarely used for reproduction.

Needless to say, thorough understanding of these processes is essential to your professional development. Unfortunately, it is a subject within itself and is not to be dealt with in this text. It would be enormously helpful to you if you could somehow arrange a tour through a quality commercial photo lab as well as a platemaking lab.

TWO-COLOR PROCESS

This is original art or photography prepared in tone combinations of any two colors, **usually** black and a second color. The procedure for preparing two-color process plates is similar to that for four-color process color separation. A filter is used in photographing the art to separate one color from the other, producing two continuous tone negatives, each containing the values and intensities of its respective color.

This procedure is much more involved than most artists imagine. To begin with if the art is a rendering in black and blue (or any other color), the separator can filter out the blue to obtain the black tone negative, but there is no filter for **black.** In other words, he cannot shoot the art for the blue content because he cannot filter out the black. Therefore he must, in many instances, treat the art as he would a duotone or fake two-color process job (see page 108).

Through skill and technical knowledge of the use of filters, masks, exposures and hand work on the negative, the separator contrives a negative for the blue plate. This is difficult and can be fairly expensive.

A word of advice should be heeded here. If you should be working with a black and white photograph and decide to run it as a two-color process job, you more than likely would have a retoucher retouch the second color into the photo, thus preparing a **two-color original.**

Although this is common practice, it is for the most part impractical due to the procedure just described. In essence you started out with the black tone art and added the second color, and the platemaker must separate them again.

If this procedure is followed because seeing the second color effect **before** reproduction is vital, then it is justified. But — in order to ensure better results — it may be helpful to have two matching black and white photos prepared, retouch the second color on **one** and supply the platemaker with **both** photos. He will then have the art for the black plate and use the two-color photo as a guide in preparing the second color plate. The next time you are confronted with this problem consult your platemaker for advice **before** the retouching is executed.

If the subject is to be an artist's rendering in two colors, it may be wise to consider pre-separation (see page 116). This depends, of course, upon the rendering technique or style to be used. Should the nature of the subject and style be such that it **must** be rendered in two colors, be certain the illustrator prepares it properly.

FIG. 31

The original from which Fig. 31 was printed was rendered as such in two colors . . . black and blue. The artist, being able to see the results of his mixtures of black (and white) and blue while working, was able to control their application. Aside from the actual experience of working in black and a color, it is not particularly difficult to control. It depends upon the approach and technique of the artist and the desired effect.

However, due to the fact that it is the **original art** that sells itself to the art director or client, there is a tendency (on the part of the artist) to **fake** the second color. If you are working in black and blue, you should use **only** the blue to be used in the printing or as close to it as possible). **Do not mix blues!** Do not use a reddish blue in one area, greenish blue in another and sky blue someplace else just to snap up the art. Remember, the ink used in printing will not change. Working in this way is likely to reproduce poor gradations in values, a muddy area here, a washed out area there . . . too strong an area someplace else. A competent artist will discipline himself; a good art director will call it to the artist's attention. For your own sake as a commercial artist, you want the best reproduction possible . . . why not do everything possible to achieve it?

In two-color process art, one color should be a light color, preferably a brilliant one to avoid muddiness and dullness. The other should be a darker or black tone to carry the detail.

FIG. 31

Using black tone as the "key plate" and **blue** as the second color warrants special consideration. Unless it is a clear, light blue, there is a tendency to grayness in tints less than 40% value, cutting down on the effectiveness of the job. Heavy underpainting of values close to the tone of the key plate (regardless of color) has a tendency to become muddy and dull in reproduction.

Artists sometimes blame the printer if a job is not satisfactory. Admittedly, the reproduction processes have their limitations, but **think** . . . perhaps the fault lies in the preparation of the art work.

Incidentally, do not get the impression that green, for example, can only be produced by printing yellow and blue. Any color can be premixed by the printer and used in the printing. This is referred to as "matching a color" (see page 92).

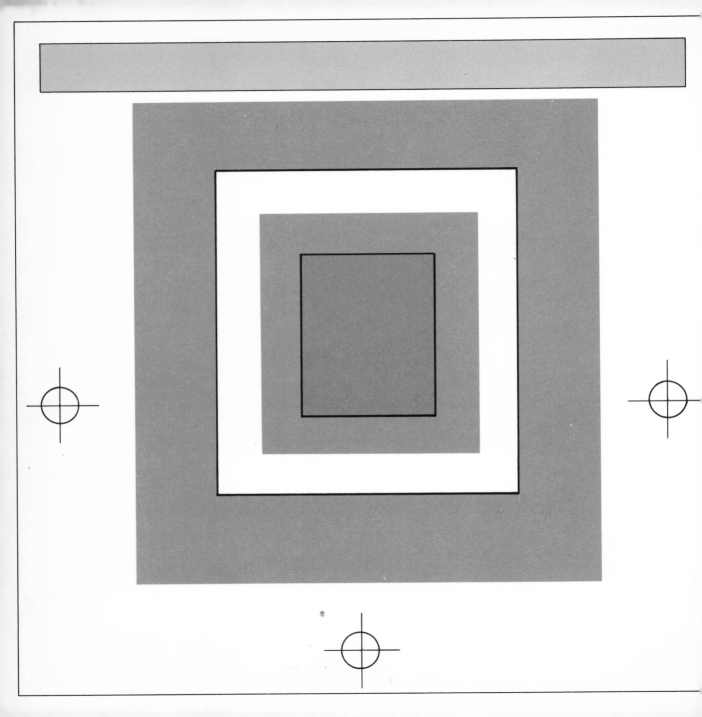

Chapter 6: Mechanical Color Separation

In this category of color separation, the original copy does not necessarily contain the colors at all. They must be **created** in a combined process of art and photography. It is not until the job is printed that the color effect is first seen; although a color sketch or dummy is made by the artist as a guide. Preparing art for this type of color printing is called "Mechanical Color Separation" and is printed in line, with screens and/or halftone combinations of color. Economy is the reason for this method of color separation.

The techniques of mechanical color separation about to be explained are used for achieving printed solid color combinations as well as screens of both color and black.

TWO-COLOR LINE ART

Your art should be prepared and designed the easiest way possible for reproduction, without interfering with the quality.

Two-color line means that two plates will be used in the printing; each for a different color.

Both color plates are line; no halftones will be used. The colors can be any combination . . . not necessarily using black as one. One of the two color plates is referred to as the "key plate." This plate generally contains the detail in the art or reading matter and it usually is the darker of the two colors for maximum effect.

It is common practice to use black and a color. This is referred to as Black and One Color. Do not be confused — it is still considered a **two color** job.

Utilization of two colors in printing can be both advantageous and desirable. It makes possible a variety of applications because there is no formula or hard and fast rules in its usage. Used properly and with thought it can give accent in a design, emphasis to a particular item; it can be used subtly or lavishly; but without proper thought and design it can produce a garish effect.

Bear in mind that this type of line art work is seldom **rendered** in the **actual colors** to be used in the printing. Seldom, because it presents a problem in the **photographic** separation of the two colors which can be expensive or impossible, i.e., if the colors are faint, light in intensity it will be very difficult to photograph for line. Colors of the same intensity used together may be impossible to separate at all. Red and black, for example, may be difficult to filter.

The important thing to remember is that reproduction is the ultimate goal. There are a number of expedient techniques, materials and methods used in color separation. The artist's skill, combined with his knowledge of plate-making methods, has the greatest influence upon the quality of the printed result.

There are essentially two categories of art preparation for color separation: "Indication" of the colors and "Separation" of the colors.

KEYLINE INDICATION

Color "indication" can be done by using the **outline** method. This is done by preparing the art in black and white for one color and outlining the boundaries of the second color areas in red directly in position on the art. This red outline is referred to by a number of expressions such as "keyline," "holding line" or "guideline." For the sake of simplification we will use the term "keyline" in this text.

To the film stripper a red keyline indicates the shape and boundaries of a solid or screened tint color area. The **line** itself, although it will appear on the negative, is **not** to be printed. Because the meaning of a red keyline by itself is ambiguous, as you will see further along in the text, it is imperative that you indicate precisely what it represents.

This is done on tracing tissue, taped over the art, using colored pencils, pastel or color markers representing the second color (or both colors) to be used in the printing. Bear in mind that this is simply an indication of the color and does not have to be an absolute match. The exact color is the printer's responsibility.

While the tissue (containing the color indication) is called a "color break," "color breakdown" or "color indication" it is often confused with the term "overlay." The "color

FIG. 32

Red keyline   Black line art

THIS AREA TO PRINT SOLID BLUE

Tissue over art (color break)

break" tissue should **not** be called an **"overlay."** It is merely a means of identifying color areas for the printer and not to be used as art for reproduction. Primarily an "overlay" refers to art of some sort to be used for reproduction (see page 72).

FIG. 32

A thin red line is drawn on the art to indicate the boundaries of the second color area. In this case the second color is to be printed as a solid color over the black line art. A tissue is placed over the art and the second color area (only) is colored in on this tissue with instructions to the printer to print the red outlined area in solid color over the black art.

This is an elementary use of the second color.

FIG. 33

Translucent ruby film
on clear base

Film stripper places
register marks on art

Surface
peeled away;
exposing clear
film base

Stripper
cuts along
keyline

Perhaps it would be advantageous at this time to suggest a formula approach to analyze the preparation of art. First, always work **backwards:** that is, from the printing press back to the art work, i.e.—printing plate, negative, camera, art.

Now how does the printer use the art when prepared with a keyline? Working backwards,

he needs **two** plates, one for the black and one for the blue. In order to produce these plates, he needs **two** negatives. The negatives are to be **line** negatives—**clear image** (the image to be printed) on black film.

Now in order to produce the clear image on a line negative the photo platemaker needs **black** art in the **complete shape** of the image.

FIG. 34

FILM NEGATIVE

Ruby shape recorded as a
clear shape on black film

The color shape as it will appear
by itself when plated and printed

All he has to work with in this instance is the complete art for the black plate but just an **outline** for the blue plate—he needs the **complete shape** or **mass** in order to produce a printing plate. Therefore he must **create** it.

FIG. 33

There are a number of techniques used by the stripper at this point. One of the simplest would be to place a ruby colored film over the art and prepare a mask for the second color. This colored film consists of a sheet of clear Mylar (or similar substance) coated with a thin layer of ruby colored rubber-like material which can be cut and peeled from the surface. The shape remaining on the surface is the area to be printed in the second color. This is the printer's "overlay" or "mask."

FIG. 35

FILM NEGATIVE — Red keyline recorded on negative as a clear line.

Keyline is opaqued before making the black plate

FIG. 34

A sheet of white paper is placed beneath the overlay, consequently blocking out all that is on the board. The image on the overlay is ruby (deep red) in color and photographs as black would, creating a clear shape on the negative. This negative will be used to make the second color plate.

FIG. 35

The overlay is lifted back and the base plate is photographed for the first color.

Note that the red line is also recorded on the negative as a clear line. If this line were left on the negative during plating, it would reproduce

64

The black as it will appear by itself when plated and printed

Using the register marks as a guide, both plates are printed one over the other in perfect alignment. Register marks are trimmed off after printing.

as a black line. However, this line is not meant to be printed (that is why it is drawn in red) and must be opaqued (blacked out) on the negative.

Each film is then separately exposed to metal and developed onto printing plates, one for each color. Both colors are then printed one over the other in perfect registration.

Realize that the printing plates are simply surfaces to carry the ink. It is your instructions that tell the printer which plate is to print in whatever color you require: in this instance we want the second color to print 100% blue.

65

FIG. 36

FIG. 37

Screened tint of blue

Keyline prints black

FIG. 36

To carry this one step further, the second color can be printed as a screened tint rather than solid. No change in the art is necessary. All you have to do is indicate the percent of screen on the tissue color break. The stripper will then strip a screened negative over the clear area on the negative. When printed it will appear as a lighter value of the second color.

FIG. 37

If you wanted the second color to be outlined by the first, the keyline would then have to be **black.** Now you must be certain that the stripper understands that the black line is your keyline for the second color **as well as** a black line to be printed around it.

FIG. 38

FIG. 39

Desired effect

Black line of art acts as keyline
for second color to butt.

Red keyline defines shape where
two colors do not butt.

FIG. 38

Suppose the design calls for only portions of the second color to be outlined by the first.

FIG. 39

The art is prepared with a red keyline along the outside boundaries (only where no black lines will butt the second color). This, however, is not enough for the stripper. The complete color shape must be filled in on a tissue over the art, showing precisely where the second color is to butt the first.

FIG. 40

FILM NEGATIVE

Red keyline develops as clear—
the same as the black lines.

A

Keyline deleted
(to be used for the black plate)

FIG. 40

The art is photographed, producing a film negative containing the complete drawing as a clear line on an opaque background. This film negative will be used for the black plate only. Therefore, the film stripper will delete those lines which were done in red on the art, leaving only the lines to be printed in black. The black plate can be made from this negative.

Now what about the second color? The platemaker needs a film containing clear areas of the shape to be printed in blue. The film negative cannot be used because it only contains a clear outline.

FIG. 41

FILM POSITIVE

Made from the film negative
(black lines on a clear film)

FIG. 42

All areas opaqued on the positive,
leaving clear shapes which are to be
printed in the second color.

FIG. 41

At this point it should be understood that the
film stripper can use a ruby film and cut a
mask (as described on page 60) or work with
a **film positive** made from the film negative
before opaquing the keyline.

FIG. 42

How would a film positive be used? The stripper opaques those areas to be printed in black,
leaving clear shapes of the areas to be printed
in blue.

Each film (Fig. 40A and Fig. 42) is then exposed to separate printing plates.

FIG. 43

DESIRED EFFECT

FIG. 44

ART PREPARATION
(no red keyline)

FIG. 43

Should the design be such that the entire second color area is to be outlined by black, you do **not** outline it in **red.** It should be done in black for the black plate. A very carefully prepared color break tissue over the art should explain where the second color is to print.

Remember, the red line is a signal to the platemaker that the line should be **deleted** after it serves its purpose. **The line itself is not to be printed.**

FIG. 44

In this case the drawing for the black plate is also used as the keyline for the second color. All that is required is the initial drawing and an accurate color break tissue as described in Fig. 43.

FILM NEGATIVE
To be used for the black plate

FILM POSITIVE
Opaqued, to be used for the color plate
(as in Fig. 42)

From the standpoint of the artist the outline method is an ideal way to prepare art of this nature, but all the separation work must be done by the film stripper. For the most part this is little trouble with simple art work. The film negative for both the offset and letterpress (photoengraving) plate is the familiar acetate type. It can be cut apart or combined with another negative, revised and restripped with little or no trouble at all, depending on the effect desired. If the desired effect is quite involved, this simple method of indicating color separation should be discarded and the art should be prepared by the use of overlays.

SEPARATION OVERLAYS

The artist actually prepares the two color plates as **separate pieces** of art that are photographed individually with no further work required of the film stripper aside from minor cleanup.

FIG. 45

The black plate is drawn on the board in black. The second color shape is lightly drawn in pencil rather than a red keyline. Register marks (at least 3) should be placed on the art. Be certain these marks are **outside** the live area (printing area). Then a sheet of "prepared" clear acetate is positioned over it and securely taped across the top. Note: clear acetate is available in two surfaces . . . prepared and plain. The plain will not adequately accept ink—the prepared will. Register marks are placed on the acetate in perfect alignment with those on the art. The second color areas are **completely** inked in on this acetate (overlay) in solid black.

FIG. 46

When the two pieces are shot separately, the negatives are complete and ready for plating.

When inking in the overlay, be careful and accurate where one color butts the other. Actually, there should be a very **slight overlap** (called a trap) to insure clean butting of the two colors.

If color is over-printing thin lines such as detail within the color area, it is impractical and unnecessary to ink around the lines on the overlay. Simply ink over them. However, the importance of keeping a **very thin** overlap of butting **shapes** or **masses** cannot be overemphasized.

FIG. 45

Register marks

Accurate, light pencil guideline on art.

BASE ART (for the black plate)

Area for second color inked in solid black on the acetate

Clear, prepared acetate

Register marks on acetate to match those on the art

THE OVERLAY

FIG. 46

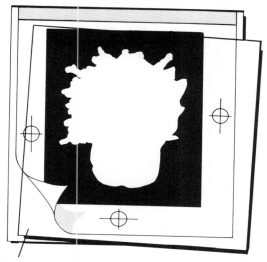

White paper is placed under the acetate (covering the base art) and a film negative is shot.

Line negative for the color plate

Line negative of the base art for the black plate.

END RESULT

FIG. 47

Needed portion of film
accidentally peeled away

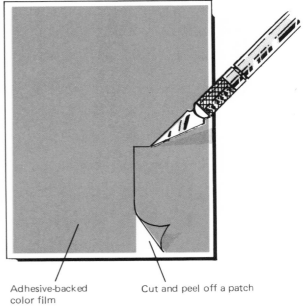

Adhesive-backed
color film

Cut and peel off a patch

COLOR FILM OVERLAYS

Another method of preparing overlays is to use a translucent color film such as the ruby film used by the film stripper (see page 60). However, you may find the ruby colored film to be too dense to see through clearly. Amber colored film seems to be the most popular with artists. It is easier to see through and photographs as sharply as ruby.

Now the purpose of a translucent color film in preparing your art overlay is primarily to save time. Inking large areas on clear acetate

could be messy and time consuming. It is also very difficult to distinguish between your black ink on the acetate and the black art beneath it, often causing errors.

If the film were black, you would not be able to see through it. Therefore, the film used for this purpose should be a translucent color of deep enough intensity to photograph as black, thus ruby, process red or amber. While this material is excellent, inasmuch as it is easy to cut and peel away, bear in mind that once it

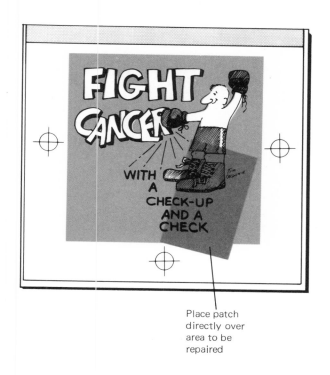

Place patch
directly over
area to be
repaired

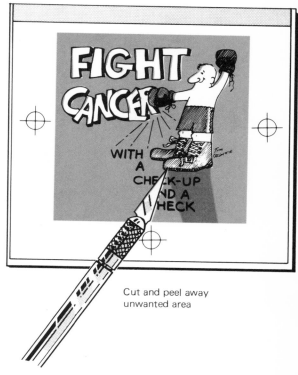

Cut and peel away
unwanted area

has been peeled off it cannot be replaced (it will not adhere). But, in the event that you should inadvertently remove an area that you should not have, it can be repaired.

FIG. 47

Sheets of adhesive-backed film are available in a number of colors, both solid and tinted. Use a solid process red or orange for the repair. It does not have to match the color film you are repairing. You simply cut a piece large enough to overlap the area to be patched, place it

directly over the film on the overlay, burnish lightly and re-cut along the proper edge. Peel away the unwanted area. Do not be concerned with the difference in color of the overlapped area. To the camera it is all the same. After completion of the repair, burnish the patch firmly in position.

If the area to be repaired is very small, it can be repaired by painting over it with black acetate ink or photographer's red opaque paint.

FIG. 48

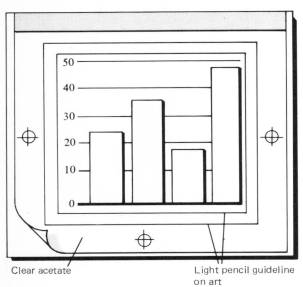

Clear acetate   Light pencil guideline
                                 on art

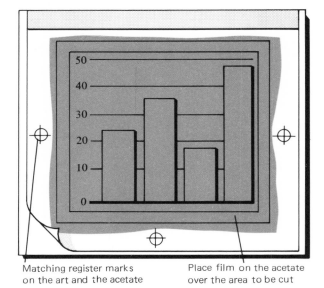

Matching register marks   Place film on the acetate
on the art and the acetate   over the area to be cut

FIG. 48

At times using this kind of prepared overlay film may not be practical. If this is so, you can prepare your own overlay using the adhesive-backed film just described.

Lightly pencil a guide line on the art representing the extremes of the color shape. Place register marks on the art in at least three places; usually one on each side and one at the top or bottom. Be certain these register marks are outside (about a quarter inch or so) the live area (the area to be done on the overlay). Now place a sheet of plain, clear acetate (or prepared) over the art. Tape it securely across the top to the full width. Cut the tape flush with the edges of the acetate so that it can lie flat if flipped up and back.

Place register marks on the acetate to align (absolutely) with those on the art. Cut and peel away enough of the red adhesive-backed film to cover the area you need for the second color. Place it carefully onto the acetate over the proper area. Burnish lightly with your hand to push out all the air from beneath to avoid large air pockets, creases, and bubbles.

If bubbles do remain, they can be punctured with a push pin or blade. Press around the bubble toward the puncture to push the air out. Do not burnish too firmly at this time or it may be difficult to lift the excess pieces. Burnish well **after** completion.

Using a well sharpened X-acto or new razor blade, carefully and gently cut along the edges

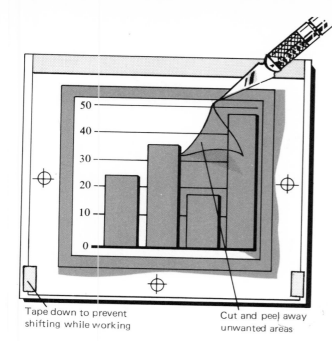

Tape down to prevent
shifting while working

Cut and peel away
unwanted areas

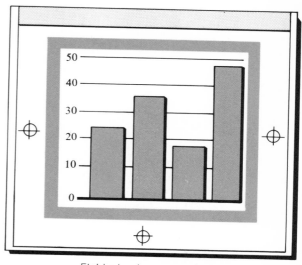

Finished, color separated art

representing the second color. Realize that cutting this material (as well as the prepared film) can be disastrous if you press too hard while cutting. Apply just enough pressure to cut **only** the colored film — not through the acetate as well. This can be achieved in a short time with a little practice. Peel away the unwanted portions. Place a sheet of tracing tissue on top of the overlay (for protection) and burnish firmly.

Note that, unlike the prepared films, this material, if lifted, will re-adhere if replaced. That's an advantage! However, in all fairness, it should be brought to your attention that the prepared overlay films do have their advantages. They are much easier to cut and peel

away and have no bubbles or creases to contend with. On the other hand the adhesive-backed films are much more difficult to peel away after cutting.

Whether the overlay is ruby, amber or red, it will photograph as though it were black. Therefore, if you should have to repair the overlay (as previously described), you can also use black ink for the repair if it will stick to the acetate. It may look strange (the black ink and the red film) but the camera doesn't see the difference — it will still photograph as if it were **all** black. By the same token be sure you do not place your black register marks **on** the color film. You may be able to see them, but the camera cannot!

Chapter 7: Overlay vs. Keyline

Actually a simplified definition of color separation by the artist means **creating art to be photographed for plating.** What the platemaker needs, and the material with which he works, determines, to a great degree, the method of art preparation.

It is obviously an impossible, if not unnecessary, task to list all the combinations of art problems. But it would be helpful to discuss a few typical color separation requirements and how they may be achieved — looking at

them through the eyes of the platemaker.

Perhaps the most important factor to consider is the negative from which the plate must be made. Always take this into account before deciding which method to use . . . the negative must have a completely clear shape of the image to be printed. If you use a **keyline** — the **platemaker** or **stripper** must somehow create art to produce the clear shape. He has his own methods, one of which is to simply prepare an overlay on the original art — or perhaps work with a film positive and opaquing paint. If you use an **overlay — you** have created the art for the clear shape, saving work for the stripper.

Regardless of who creates that master shape, it must ultimately be done in order to prepare the printing plate.

In view of this, one would conclude that the keyline method is incorrect. In a sense it is. After all, it is only a guide for someone to eventually prepare an overlay.

If these are the facts, then why bother using the keyline method at all? Simply to save time for the artist. If the image to be separated is simple, does not contain intricate detail or overlapping shapes, then you may elect to use a keyline. However, if the image is intricate or requires an artist's skill, it may be wise to prepare an overlay rather than run the risk of the stripper misjudging the meaning of a complicated keyline.

Working with type in conjunction with art or simple shapes needlessly confuses the artist. To begin with, type is essentially no different than art. It is just a different configuration. For example, the art in Fig. 48 contains type (the numerals). If you wanted the type to print in the second color, it could be pasted on the **overlay** along with the shapes.

FIG. 49

Here we have a simple mechanical with type and a color. Note that except for the fact that the base art is type, this problem is no different than that of Fig. 32. The art can be prepared using either a keyline or an overlay.

FIG. 49

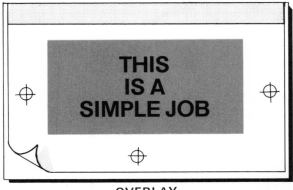

A
DESIRED EFFECT

KEYLINE

OVERLAY

B

D

C

E

However, in B the color shape overlaps a portion of the black shape. To use a red keyline for this would be impractical. It would look like C. Note that the red line becomes a problem. In this case it would be better to simply prepare an overlay. Remember, the red keyline must be opaqued from the negative. If it is drawn over the black portions, it becomes extremely difficult to do so. This should be avoided.

In D we have an even more obvious reason not to use a keyline. It would look like E.

As a side note in defense of the keyline, there is a way to use it on complicated jobs such as this. **The keyline could be drawn on an overlay.** In other words the **overlay does not have to contain a solid mass of the shape.** Suppose you did not have access to proper material to prepare an actual overlay. You could use a sheet of vellum, tracing paper, prepared acetate (anything that you could draw on) and draw a red (or even a black) keyline on it as an overlay. The platemaker will then follow your keyline as he would if it had been drawn on the art itself. As a rule this is seldom done.

But let's look into the various combinations.

FIG. 50

A
DESIRED EFFECT

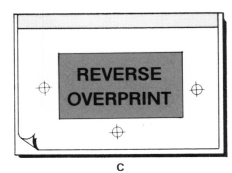

B
Base art

C
Film stripper's ruby overlay

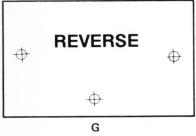

G
Film positive made from
negative assembly **F**

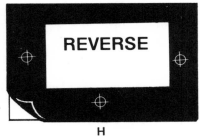

H
Film negative **D** placed over
film positive **G** and exposed
to plate for blue

Blue plate printed by itself

FIG. 50

How would you prepare your art for A?

If you used a keyline as in B, the platemaker would place register marks on the art and cut a ruby overlay of the color shape (C). He would then shoot a film negative of the overlay (D).

The overlay is lifted up and out of the way and a film negative is made of the base art (E).

Until now you have been told that the film stripper opaques unwanted areas on the negative. That is only one of the methods. However, on simple jobs he has the option to use a "masking" material called "goldenrod." This is a dense, golden colored paper that can be cut and taped over areas of a negative, a simplified method of blocking out unwanted areas, rather than taking the time to paint them out.

Using goldenrod as a mask on the negative, the stripper covers everything but the register marks and the copy to be reversed on the color plate (F). A **film positive** will be made

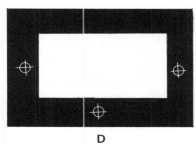

D

Film negative made from overlay **C**

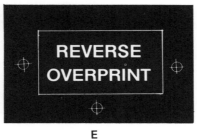

E

Film negative made from base art

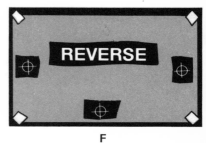

F

Goldenrod over negative **E**

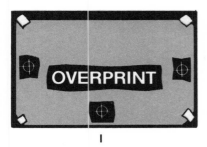

I

Goldenrod over negative **E**
and exposed to plate for black

Black plate printed by itself

PRINTED RESULT

from this assembly containing only the register marks and the copy to be reversed (G). This film positive is then combined (contacted) with the film negative of the color shape and exposed to a plate (H). The end result is the color shape with white (reversed) type.

Just a reminder at this point — the type appears white because the pages in this book are white — if the pages were orange, the type would be orange on a color background. So, "reverse" does not in itself mean "white."

Let's get back to the film negative of the base art (F). The stripper removes the goldenrod mask and cuts a new one covering everything but the register marks and the type to print black (I). This negative is exposed to a plate. The end result is the black type by itself.

When both plates are printed one over the other, it will produce the specified effect.

FIG. 51

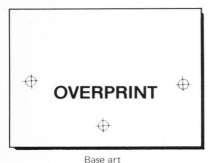

Base art

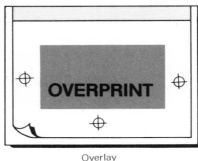

Overlay

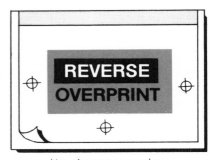

Negative stat on overlay

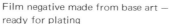

Film negative made from base art —
ready for plating

Film negative made from overlay —
ready for plating

FIG. 51

In Fig. 50 the art was prepared with a keyline. Using this approach, the platemaker does most of the work . . . and charges for it.

Now let's consider using an overlay instead of a keyline. As a general rule, once you decide to use an overlay it should be as complete as possible for the platemaker.

The specifications call for copy to reverse on the color plate. Your overlay represents the color plate—to make it complete you should

also reverse the copy. Simply paste up a negative stat directly on the red film. Be sure to blacken the white edges of the stat before pasting it on the overlay or else it will record on the platemaker's negative as a black line.

All the platemaker has to do is shoot a negative of the base art and one of the overlay. Aside from minor clean up (called spotting) on the negatives, he has all he needs at this time to make plates.

Compare this method of preparation with that of Fig. 50. In the long run this may be a little more work for you, but much less for the platemaker. The more thoroughly familiar you are with the material and supplies available to the artist, as well as the procedure used by the film stripper or platemaker, the simpler it will be for all concerned.

Whether you are doing a mechanical or preparing art work, a question often asked is, "how shall I prepare this art? Should I use an overlay or a keyline?" The nature of the art, the method of reproduction and the printed effect required usually dictate the answer. Actually there are no hard and fast rules in color separation . . . just common sense.

PROCESS COLOR PRINTING INKS

There are two main categories of color printing: Process Color Printing and Standard (or) Matched Color Printing. In process color printing three standard **transparent** color inks are used — magenta, yellow and cyan (more commonly referred to as red, yellow and blue) in conjunction with black. By printing combinations of these four colors in both screen tints and solids, literally hundreds of colors can be produced.

This can be confusing, however, when preparing mechanical separations. In Chapter 5, we discussed the production of four color process plates (halftone). This method of preparing plates must be used because the original was prepared in full color. The printer, in this case, has the original to follow as a guide for matching colors. But when you prepare **mechanically separated art** you must specify to the film stripper the screen tint and/or solid

combinations of colors he must use to create the color you require.

To recapitulate, the platemaker needs a line negative with a **clear shape** of the image to be printed. The best color to use for a sharp clear image is black, deep red, (ruby), solid process red, solid orange or amber. The art is simply a means of creating the surface shape on the printing plate. That surface can carry any color ink the printer chooses to put in the press.

Because the adhesive-backed colored films are available in varying values of each color, it may be misleading to the beginner. For example, if an area is to be printed in light blue, you may think a light blue film should be used for the overlay. This is wrong inasmuch as it may not photograph properly for line plating.

When printing in line we have the option to print solid (100%) color or screened tints of that color. As shown in Fig. 36, the overlay used for **solid color** can **also** be used for a **screened tint of color.**

The clear shape on the line negative can be broken down into a screened (dot) formation by placing a film of dots over it while plating. This will, when printed, appear as a lighter value (tint) of the color.

Without changing the art, by simply changing the instructions to the printer, both base art and/or the overlay can be printed in any two colors you specify . . . red and blue; green and black; orange and brown, etc. Therefore, the determining factor is neither the color of the original art nor the color used for the overlay, but the **instructions** you give the photo platemaker or printer.

FIG. 52

DESIRED EFFECT

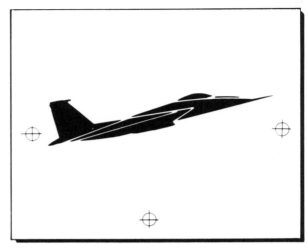

Base art for black plate

FIG. 52

For example: in Fig. 52 the second color indication is for solid blue. If you wanted a tint of blue you would have to clearly indicate the percent screen for the film stripper. There would be no need to prepare the art differently — just your instructions. The film stripper would simply apply (strip) the proper screen negative over the clear area on the negative before plating and the printed result would be a lighter blue.

If a screen **tint** of color is required and you use a color film **tint** for your overlay, for example, a 30% value of blue, the cameraman must use a filtering system in order to pick it up as **line copy**. In itself, it is not intense enough to be recorded by the camera. Tints of certain colors such as 10% blue, red or yellow cannot be filtered for **line** and would have to be shot in **halftone**. To repeat, should you want to use a tint of color film as the overlay, it is advisable to consult your production manager or platemaker first.

Sometimes the mechanical or art is prepared in this manner to permit the client to visualize the end result more clearly and perhaps make revisions. After approval, the overlay is then **redone** with black or red color film.

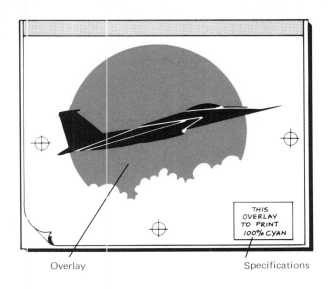

Overlay   Specifications

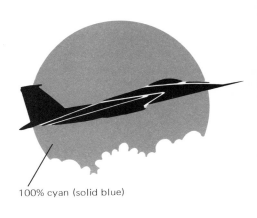

100% cyan (solid blue)

PRINTED RESULT

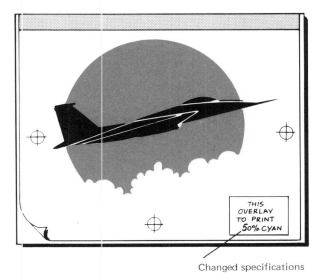

Changed specifications

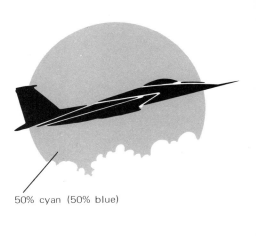

50% cyan (50% blue)

PRINTED RESULT

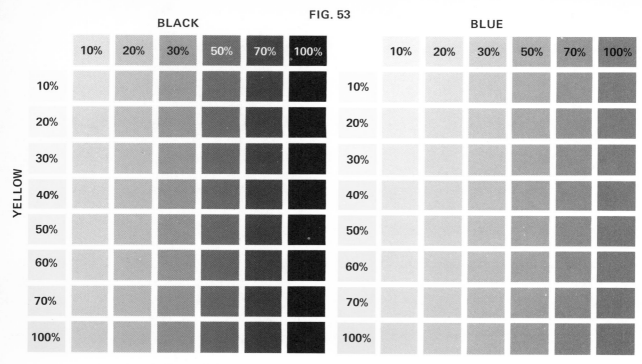

A portion of a Process Color Chart showing combinations of black and yellow and of blue and yellow

FIG. 53

But suppose you wanted the second color to be **green** instead of blue? Now — Ha-Ha — without realizing it, you have changed the printing specifications from a **two**-color job to a **three**-color job. In order to create green, you need to print **blue** and **yellow** in that area. Thus you're printing with three colors — **black, blue** and **yellow.** Your budget will only allow printing two colors. What does this mean? It means that if the job is being printed with process colors and all your budget will allow is two colors — you cannot request

black and green. But if you are willing to compromise on the shade or hue of green, there may be hope. For example, if you refer to a **Process Color Ink Chart** you will see greens created by tints of black and yellow. You could print the job in **black** and **yellow** and achieve black and green.

Or you could print blue (instead of black) and yellow to get a different green. The line work would be blue . . . that may create other problems . . . but cheer up! It isn't hopeless.

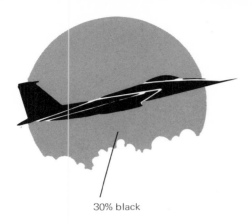

30% black

100% yellow

100% yellow over 30% black
(2 colors)

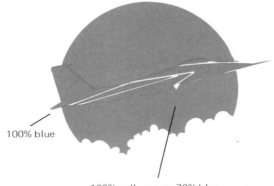

100% blue

100% yellow over 70% blue
(2 colors)

89

FIG. 54

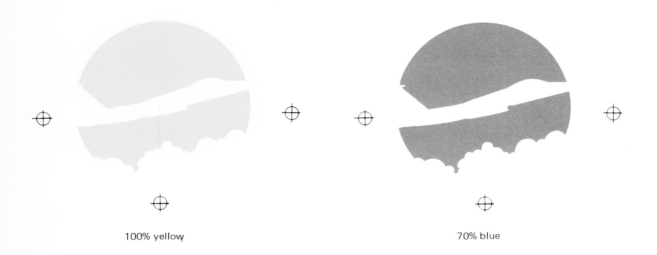

100% yellow   70% blue

FIG. 54

If, after all, you do intend to print with 3 colors (blue, yellow and black), shouldn't a **separate overlay** be prepared for **each** color? Basically, that is true if each color has a different shape. But when you have a particular shape or area requiring two or more colors to achieve the color you want, one overlay is all that is necessary.

Find the particular shade of green you want on the Process Color Ink Chart, read the code for the color, i.e., 30% blue and 40% yellow, 70% blue and 100% yellow, etc., and indicate that code on your art.

Using the one negative, made from the overlay, the platemaker will expose it to a plate for yellow. Then, the film stripper will apply a screen over the negative and prepare a second plate for 70% blue. When both plates

90

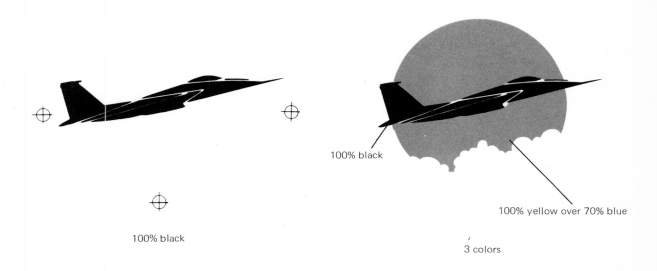

100% black

100% black

100% yellow over 70% blue

3 colors

(which carry identical shapes) are printed one over the other in their respective colors, the result will be the shade of green you have chosen from the chart.

You will usually come in contact with the restrictions of process color when printing in magazines, periodicals, books, etc. This book, for example, was printed in process. Publication presses are set up for process printing in order to reproduce four color effects for their ads and editorials. Some publications do offer special colors for two color jobs. These are referred to as Standard Green, Orange, Red, etc., for which they charge extra. The best thing to do is consult your production manager or the publication for exact specifications.

A simulated reproduction of matched color swatches.   **FIG. 55**

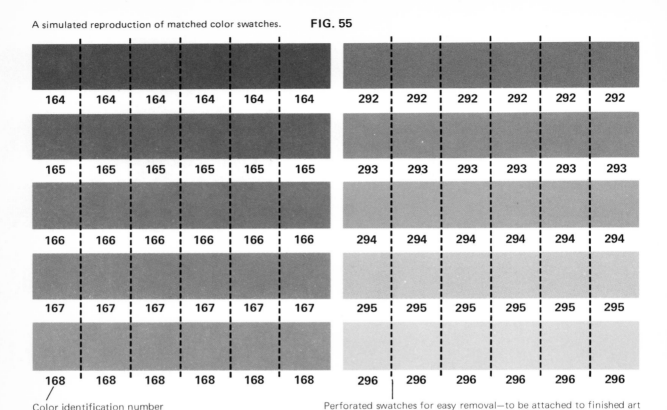

164	164	164	164	164	164
165	165	165	165	165	165
166	166	166	166	166	166
167	167	167	167	167	167
168	168	168	168	168	168

292	292	292	292	292	292
293	293	293	293	293	293
294	294	294	294	294	294
295	295	295	295	295	295
296	296	296	296	296	296

Color identification number

Perforated swatches for easy removal—to be attached to finished art

MATCHED COLOR INKS

When printing special promotional pieces such as mailing folders, posters, brochures, annual reports, etc., you have more flexibility when using color. Because you will use a private printer for this kind of work, you can request the specific color ink to be printed. This is referred to as "Matched Color."

FIG. 55

Printers' colored ink swatch books are available displaying several hundred color hues

and tints to choose from; each color is coded for identification. You simply instruct the printer to print the job using a specific color.

Now there are two very serious considerations when using these matched colors. One is the stock (paper) it will print on. Take special note when viewing the swatch book — it should contain two sections — both of which show the same colors printed on different stock.

One section will be on a coated stock (glossy), the other on uncoated (matte) stock. The dif-

92

ference in the richness and vitality of the color is staggering. Be absolutely certain you consider the stock while choosing the color ink or you may ruin the job.

The next important consideration is the results you expect when printing a screened tint of the matched color. Not all charts show screened tints of matched colors. For example, what would a 30% screen of #166 in Fig. 55 look like? How would it look on coated stock vs. uncoated? Furthermore, what would 30% of #166 printed over #296 look like? Be cautious!

One more tip that may be helpful: if you do not have access to a color chart or cannot find a particular color on the chart, you can paint your own swatch and have the printer mix inks to match it (as closely as he can).

FIG. 56

Generally speaking, the base art represents the black plate, and the overlay is for the second color. This may be due to the fact that most two-color jobs are black and a color; the black plate, usually carrying the detail, may be more involved. In other words the more complicated plate is done on the board because it is more convenient. But there is no stringent rule dictating which portion of the job is to be done on the board or the overlay. The nature of each job will determine this—you must be the judge.

For example, using the same art assembly as in Fig. 52, we can change the color plates by simply changing the specifications to the printer. The results — most anything you want . . .

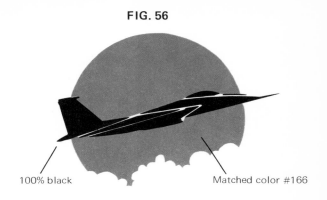

FIG. 56

100% black

Matched color #166

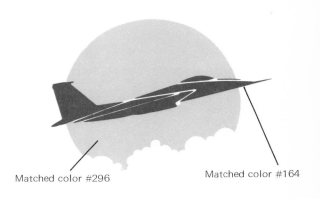

Matched color #296

Matched color #164

100% black

50% red over 10% blue over 20% black   (process colors)

FIG. 57

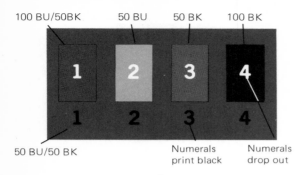

100 BU/50BK   50 BU   50 BK   100 BK

50 BU/50 BK   Numerals   Numerals
print black   drop out

A

SPECIFICATIONS

B

Keyline for all shapes with black type

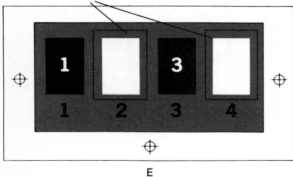

Piece of white paper under ruby overlay

E

Board is shot as-is through the ruby overlay

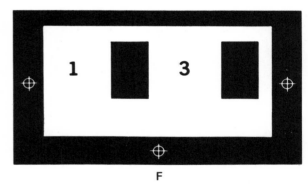

F

Film negative of **E** to be used for 50% black

FIG. 57

Study the specifications (A) in Fig. 57 before continuing with the procedure that follows. The specifications are: 2 colors — black and blue; the background will carry a 50% tint of black as well as a 50% tint of blue; bar 1 will print 100% blue over 50% black; bar 2 will contain only 50% blue; bar 3 only 50% black; and bar 4 only 100% black. The numerals in the bars will drop out; the numerals beneath the bars will print black.

Now ask yourself — "how should I prepare the art for this?" It could be done completely with red keylines as in B. Perhaps it could be done with overlays — if so — how many? Are overlays necessary?

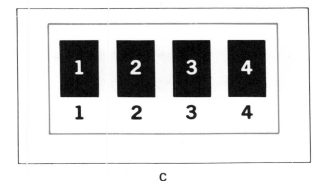

C

Combination of black shapes and type
with keyline — no overlay

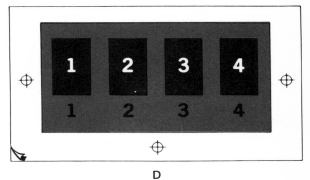

D

Film stripper applies register marks
and cuts ruby overlay

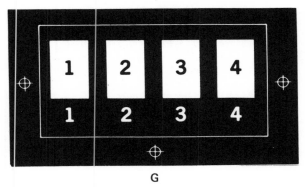

G

Film negative of base art **C**

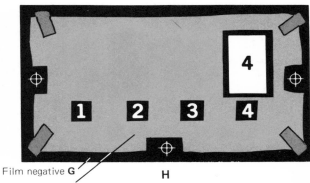

Film negative **G**

H

Goldenrod blocks out all but the area to print 100% black

Why not do all the art directly in position on the board? The shapes are simple enough and do not overlap or intertwine. It could be prepared using a combination of a red keyline and solid blacks ... why not? It would look like C. Place a tissue over art C and prepare a color break with instructions (specifications) as in A. Now carefully examine the procedure employed to meet these specifications. You'll realize, as you study these steps, that it may be easier for the platemaker to create certain effects than it would be for the artist. The step-by-step sequence shown here may not necessarily be precisely the order in which the film stripper would approach it, but it does depict his methods.

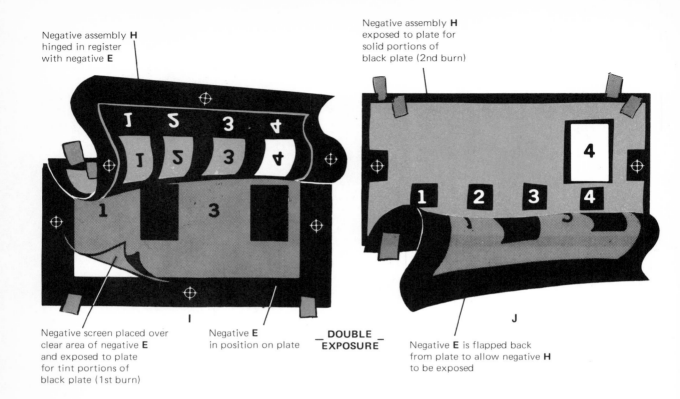

Negative assembly **H** hinged in register with negative **E**

Negative assembly **H** exposed to plate for solid portions of black plate (2nd burn)

Negative screen placed over clear area of negative **E** and exposed to plate for tint portions of black plate (1st burn)

Negative **E** in position on plate

I

Negative **E** is flapped back from plate to allow negative **H** to be exposed

J

DOUBLE EXPOSURE

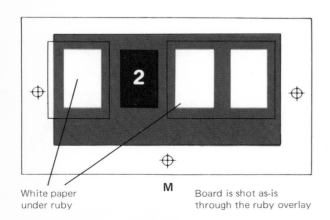

White paper under ruby

M

Board is shot as-is through the ruby overlay

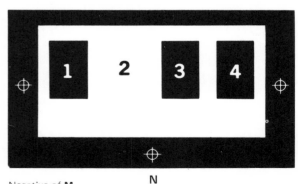

Negative of **M** to be used for 50% blue

N

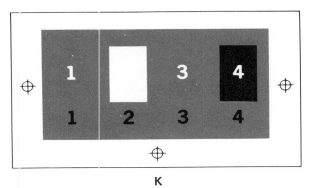

K
Result
(Black plate when printed by itself)

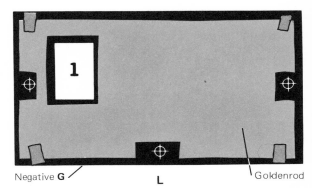

Negative **G** **L** Goldenrod

The goldenrod is removed from assembly **H** and negative is re-masked — blocking out all but the areas to print 100% blue

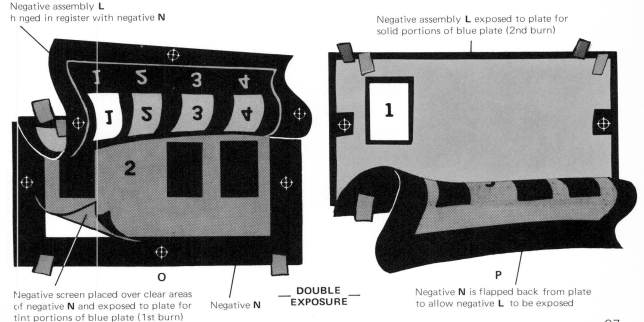

Negative assembly **L** hinged in register with negative **N**

Negative assembly **L** exposed to plate for solid portions of blue plate (2nd burn)

O

Negative screen placed over clear areas of negative **N** and exposed to plate for tint portions of blue plate (1st burn)

Negative **N**

DOUBLE EXPOSURE

P

Negative **N** is flapped back from plate to allow negative **L** to be exposed

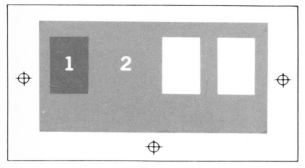

Result
(Blue plate when printed by itself)

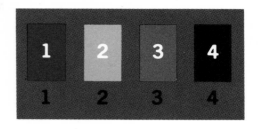

FINAL RESULT

Both plates printed in register one over the other

Mechanical color separation is actually a combination of the efforts of the artist, film stripper and platemaker. Using film negatives and positives in conjunction with goldenrod, stripping techniques and multiple exposures, the technicians can often be more precise than the artist. What is of utmost importance is how you prepare your art in accordance with the specifications. If what you specify is absolutely clear, and your art is clean and precise, you should have no trouble.

The tools, material and techniques at your disposal are subject to your imagination. By using your knowledge and understanding of repro-

duction methods you can create an infinite variety of color effects.

Whether you use a keyline, a solid black shape or an overlay is not always the most important decision in art preparation. What is vital to the assurance of the correct end result is your **clarity of specifications**.

Once again a reminder — ask yourself the questions," what is the effect I am looking for? . . . how can I make it clear to the printer? . . . what does the printer need? . . . what does the cameraman need? . . ." It could go on and on. The important thing is to think it out before getting into the preparation. You'll find

FIG. 58

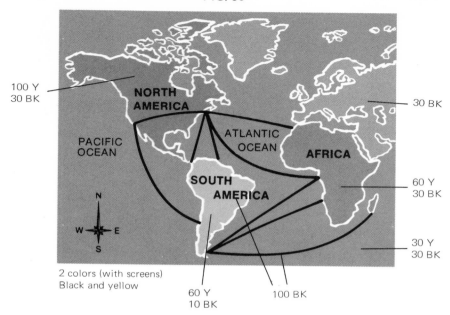

100 Y
30 BK

NORTH AMERICA

PACIFIC OCEAN

ATLANTIC OCEAN

AFRICA

30 BK

SOUTH AMERICA

60 Y
30 BK

N
W — E
S

30 Y
30 BK

2 colors (with screens)
Black and yellow

60 Y
10 BK

100 BK

that sometimes it takes longer to decide the best method of preparation than it takes to actually prepare the art, and by the same token it may take two days to prepare something it only took two minutes to figure out.

Now that you are familiar with the film stripper's and platemaker's techniques, let's look at the art from the artist's point of view. By applying what you have learned from the preceding pages, you can now create more elaborate color effects. As you study the following illustrations, use your imagination regarding the film stripper's and platemaker's role in its production.

Because printing inks are transparent, they create additional colors when printed one over the other, which means that a two-color job can produce three colors and variations of those colors. Obviously, printing with three colors multiplies the combinations and four colors could keep you busy for a long time.

Study Fig. 58 for awhile before turning this page. How would you prepare the art for it? Would you prepare overlays? How many? Red keylines? How do you prepare the art for the white lines? The black lines?

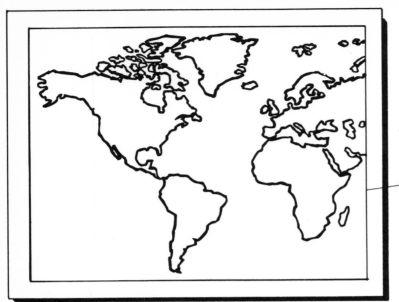

—Guideline for trim

Original drawing — black on white

Glossy negative stat made from original

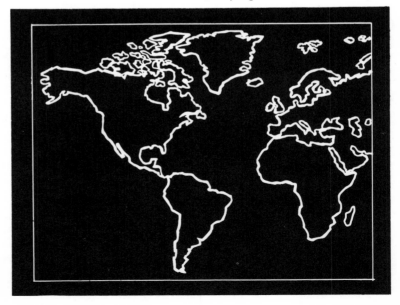

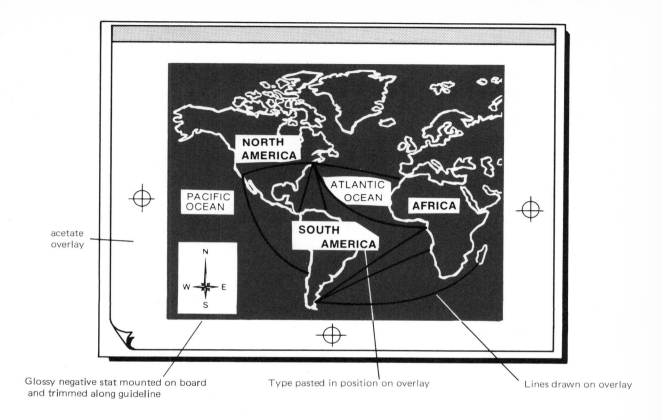

acetate
overlay

Glossy negative stat mounted on board
and trimmed along guideline

Type pasted in position on overlay

Lines drawn on overlay

ART PREPARATION

The most important consideration is to present the printer with the most you can give him to work with. Note that in this art the line work between the masses acts as a keyline. As long as the stripper has a definite line to follow, the keyline does not have to be red or black . . . it could just as easily be white. By the use of masking and stripping techniques the stripper will create the effects you specify. In this instance your color break and instructions are significantly important.

To fully separate this type of art, using overlays with any degree of accuracy would be extremely difficult and unnecessary for the artist. However, it would be comparatively easy for the film stripper to prepare it. Study the art assembly above. What can the film stripper do more accurately and easily than the artist? How does he create the various plates from the art as it was prepared? Can other color combinations be produced without changing the art? Of course!

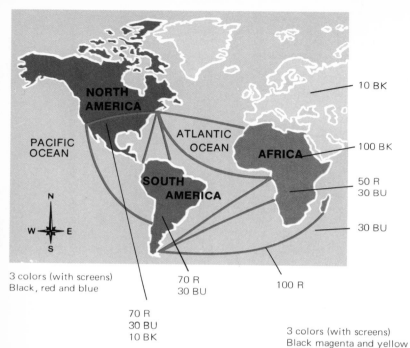

10 BK

100 BK

50 R
30 BU

30 BU

NORTH AMERICA

ATLANTIC OCEAN

PACIFIC OCEAN

AFRICA

SOUTH AMERICA

3 colors (with screens)
Black, red and blue

70 R
30 BU

100 R

70 R
30 BU
10 BK

3 colors (with screens)
Black magenta and yellow

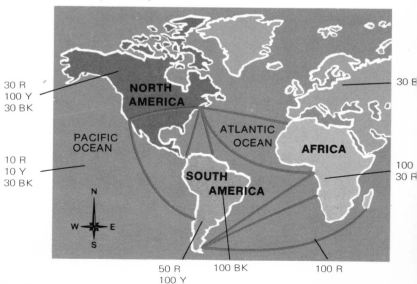

30 R
100 Y
30 BK

10 R
10 Y
30 BK

NORTH AMERICA

ATLANTIC OCEAN

PACIFIC OCEAN

AFRICA

SOUTH AMERICA

30 B

100
30 R

50 R
100 Y

100 BK

100 R

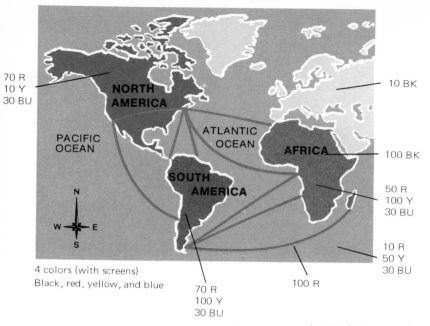

70 R
10 Y
30 BU

10 BK

PACIFIC
OCEAN

NORTH
AMERICA

ATLANTIC
OCEAN

AFRICA

100 BK

SOUTH
AMERICA

50 R
100 Y
30 BU

N
W E
S

10 R
50 Y
30 BU

4 colors (with screens)
Black, red, yellow, and blue

70 R
100 Y
30 BU

100 R

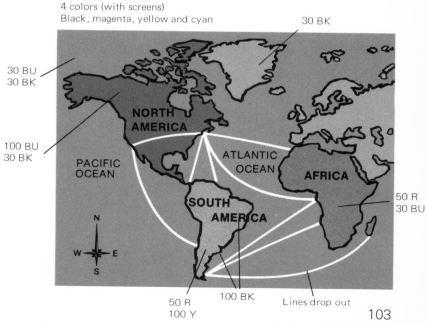

4 colors (with screens)
Black, magenta, yellow and cyan

30 BK

30 BU
30 BK

NORTH
AMERICA

100 BU
30 BK

PACIFIC
OCEAN

ATLANTIC
OCEAN

AFRICA

50 R
30 BU

SOUTH
AMERICA

N
W E
S

50 R
100 Y

100 BK

Lines drop out

103

Chapter 8:
Line and Halftone Combinations

In chapters six and seven we dealt with methods of color separation using solid colors and mechanically applied screen tints of color in order to achieve particular effects. The illustrated subject matter was essentially flat, graphic shapes, line drawings and type. Because no photos or tone illustrations were used, the plates (and printing category) were classified as **line**.

This chapter will discuss the use of halftones and line combinations. Once again a recap of two important bits of information.

In halftone, the dot formation changes in size to create tonal variations.

In line, we have no dot formation — the area is normally **solid** or full intensity of color **without variation**. The color can be varied by mechanically applying uniform dot formations (screen) on the negative, visually creating a lighter **flat** value of the color.

TWO-COLOR LINE AND HALFTONE
A popular approach to the use of two colors is successfully achieved by printing a solid or

105

FIG. 59

ORIGINAL ART

screened tint of one color over (or under) a halftone of another color. Selection of the proper color combinations is, of course, essential to pleasing results.

Preparation of color separation in this instance is in itself quite simple despite the variations of approach. Actually, the methods are much the same as in two-color line separation.

FIG. 59

Here we start out with a black and white continuous-tone photograph. We will print the photo as a black halftone, and print a solid color, or screen of color, over it. Preparation is relatively simple. For the most part you will be working with the photo in conjunction with a mechanical of some sort. You can use the keyline method along with a **photostat** of the photograph made to reproduction size. But you must be extremely careful with this method—it could be misleading (see page 111).

A word of caution: photographs are valuable pieces of art. You **must** handle them with respect .. they are often irreplaceable. There are several conditions under which you will be involved with photographs. For example, you may have to work with a loose photo. If so, avoid holding it with one hand—it could bend and crack. Cracks are almost impossible to

Solid color over black halftone

Tint of color over black halftone

remedy. It would be wise to mount the photo before working with it. However, always check with someone as to whether mounting is permissible (for whatever reason).

There are three ways to mount a photo. One is to **dry mount** it to a substantially heavy mounting board. If possible, mount it on a board with a two or three inch margin for protection or to write instructions on. The term **dry mount** is often erroneously confused with **cement mount**. Dry mount refers to mounting with a dry mount press and dry mount tissue — this is also called **hot mount**. Keep in mind that this method of mounting (if done properly) is **permanent** — once it has been

mounted, it cannot be removed without serious damage to the photo.

If for some reason you cannot mount the photo, it can be taped to a board while you are working with it for protection. Taping down just the four corners is usually all that is necessary. No matter how you use tape, be careful when removing it. You could tear the emulsion of the photo. Try wetting the tape with cement thinner before pulling it up. Before you mount the photo, be sure to check the back for information.

Another method is to **rubber cement mount** it. The print can be removed if needed.

107

FIG. 60

Black halftone

Color halftone

TWO-COLOR HALFTONE (DUOTONE)

This is perhaps the easiest type of two-color separation for the artist, because the camera-man and the platemaker do all the separation work.

You start out with a black and white contin-uous-tone photo, or illustration, and end up with what appears to be a two-color process reproduction (page 54). This is called a "duo-tone" (sometimes referred to as a duograph).

FIG. 60

Briefly, the method used here is to photo-screen the original art twice at different screen angles, as well as intensities, producing two halftone negatives. Two plates are made and the two colors are printed one over the other. Shooting duotone negatives requires skill and craftsmanship. The original must be analyzed by the cameraman before shooting the nega-tives. If the art has good contrast, with a full range of values from light to dark, you can

DUOTONE
Both colors printed one over the other

DUOTONE
Black and red

anticipate pleasing results. If the art is weak, or too strongly contrasting, you may be disappointed in the end, for it may be impossible for the cameraman to utilize effective control in his exposures.

Usually, the negative for the black plate is shot as an open (lighter) halftone to permit color to come through the dark areas, while the negative for the color plate is shot stronger than a normal halftone.

Note the difference between printing a flat color (page 105) over a black halftone as opposed to a duotone. The detail is obviously better in the duotone.

Actually a duotone can be printed in any two colors. Black does not have to be one of the colors but seems to be the most widely used and functional. Combinations of two colors other than black require a good deal of experience and understanding of color.

FIG. 61

FIG. 61

There is the possibility that you may be working with a full-color original photo, transparency or illustration and have to reproduce it as a black halftone or duotone. This will require a black and white photocopy.

Bear in mind that when we view color art, our sensitivity moves from blue through red. Our eye can differentiate values, shapes and detail in conjunction with changes in color, hue and contrast. Ordinary film used for copying is color-blind or sensitive only to ultraviolet and blue light. If this film is used, the color, converted to a gray scale, loses many subtleties of value and contrast along with detail of the subject. In order to control the gray scale during this copy conversion, a panchromatic film is used. This film is sensitive to ultraviolet, blue, green and red light. When you send the art to a photo lab, be sure to instruct them to make a **"color corrected"** copy. This type of black and white photocopy usually costs more than the normal copy print and takes longer to process.

Panchromatic color corrected photocopy

Orthochromatic black and white photocopy

111

FIG. 62

Throughout chapters six and seven, the red keyline was referred to as the boundary of, and guideline for, a color shape. When used for that purpose this is, of course, true. But the red keyline, in itself, actually has no meaning without an explanation. It can be, and in fact is, used for many things other than a color indication.

Let's take a typical one-color job containing type and a halftone. There are several methods of mechanical preparation, all of which can be debated. Nevertheless, here are the most popular approaches.

The desired effect is shown in A — type and a halftone to print in black ink — a one color job.

Under normal conditions the photograph you work with is not reproduction size. Therefore, you will have a matte stat made from the original photo to the required reproduction size. This matte stat will be pasted into proper position on the mechanical along with the type. The stat itself simply represents the required size and position of the halftone to be stripped in by the film stripper. The halftone negative, of course, is made from the original photo (see Fig. 7 for stripping methods). The controversy now is how the photostat is used in the mechanical. Here are the variations — all of which will produce the same results.

In B, the stat is trimmed to the exact dimensions required. This leaves no doubt as to what you want.

In C, a red keyline is ruled and the stat is neatly cut a fraction smaller and centered within the outline so that the red line is visible.

In D, a red keyline is ruled and the stat is cut out with a ragged (or irregular)' edge and centered within the red outline. An irregular edge is an immediate indication to the platemaker that the halftone is to butt the edge of the red boundary line.

In E, a red keyline is ruled and a simple pencil outline indication is drawn within the area. This is not a particularly popular method.

In F a red line is ruled and instructions are written within the area. Crop marks, corresponding to the red keyline shape, are drawn on the original photo (or in the margin).

Regardless of which method you use, your instructions are of utmost importance.

Now you have seen how the red keyline is used to define the boundaries of a halftone . . . it has nothing to do with a second color. This only enforces the need for specific and well defined instructions to the printer.

Any of these methods can be used to create the two-color result shown in Fig. 59. All you have to do is explain on a color break that a solid or a screen of color is to print over the black halftone. The red keyline then takes on a **different** meaning. It represents both the boundaries for the black halftone, **as well as** the second color.

It would be safe to assume that the film stripper is going to prepare his own ruby overlay following your red keyline. The reason for the red line is, to repeat, an indication to the film stripper that the color area will print as a solid (or tint) without an outline. Therefore, it will

FIG. 62

The desired effect is shown in A — type and a halftone to print in black ink — a one color job.

Under normal conditions the photograph you work with is not reproduction size. Therefore, you will have a matte stat made from the original photo to the required reproduction size. This matte stat will be pasted into proper position on the mechanical along with the type. The stat itself simply represents the required size and position of the halftone to be stripped in by the film stripper. The halftone negative, of course, is made from the original photo (see Fig. 7 for stripping methods). The controversy now is how the photostat is used in the mechanical. Here are the variations — all of which will produce the same results:

A

DESIRED EFFECT

The desired effect is shown in A — type and a halftone to print in black ink — a one color job.

Under normal conditions the photograph you work with is not reproduction size. Therefore, you will have a matte stat made from the original photo to the required reproduction size. This matte stat will be pasted into proper position on the mechanical along with the type. The stat itself simply represents the required size and position of the halftone to be stripped in by the film stripper. The halftone negative, of course, is made from the original photo (see Fig. 7 for stripping methods). The controversy now is how the photostat is used in the mechanical. Here are the variations — all of which will produce the same results:

B

The desired effect is shown in A — type and a halftone to print in black ink — a one color job.

Under normal conditions the photograph you work with is not reproduction size. Therefore, you will have a matte stat made from the original photo to the required reproduction size. This matte stat will be pasted into proper position on the mechanical along with the type. The stat itself simply represents the required size and position of the halftone to be stripped in by the film stripper. The halftone negative, of course, is made from the original photo (see Fig. 7 for stripping methods). The controversy now is how the photostat is used in the mechanical. Here are the variations — all of which will produce the same results:

C

The desired effect is shown in A — type and a halftone to print in black ink — a one color job.

Under normal conditions the photograph you work with is not reproduction size. Therefore, you will have a matte stat made from the original photo to the required reproduction size. This matte stat will be pasted into proper position on the mechanical along with the type. The stat itself simply represents the required size and position of the halftone to be stripped in by the film stripper. The halftone negative, of course, is made from the original photo (see Fig. 7 for stripping methods). The controversy now is how the photostat is used in the mechanical. Here are the variations — all of which will produce the same results:

D

The desired effect is shown in A — type and a halftone to print in black ink — a one color job.

Under normal conditions the photograph you work with is not reproduction size. Therefore, you will have a matte stat made from the original photo to the required reproduction size. This matte stat will be pasted into proper position on the mechanical along with the type. The stat itself simply represents the required size and position of the halftone to be stripped in by the film stripper. The halftone negative, of course, is made from the original photo (see Fig. 7 for stripping methods). The controversy now is how the photostat is used in the mechanical. Here are the variations — all of which will produce the same results:

E

The desired effect is shown in A — type and a halftone to print in black ink — a one color job.

Under normal conditions the photograph you work with is not reproduction size. Therefore, you will have a matte stat made from the original photo to the required reproduction size. This matte stat will be pasted into proper position on the mechanical along with the type. The stat itself simply represents the required size and position of the halftone to be stripped in by the film stripper. The halftone negative, of course, is made from the original photo (see Fig. 7 for stripping methods). The controversy now is how the photostat is used in the mechanical. Here are the variations — all of which will produce the same results:

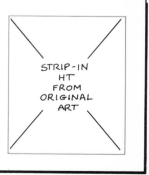

STRIP-IN HT FROM ORIGINAL ART

F

be eliminated from the negative before plating. The red line also acts as a guide for cutting his overlay. If you do not use a red line (as in B), and just cut the photostat to size, it may present a problem. When the film stripper places his ruby film over the photostat he may not be able to see the edges well enough to follow when cutting. Often, photostats wash out in light areas and the cut edges may not show. Because of this it is more advantageous to use the red keyline method. Whether you cut the photostat neatly, but smaller, or with a ragged edge is totally up to you, as long as the film stripper understands what you want him to do. For example, if you were to use method C, the neatly trimmed stat may be misinterpreted to mean that the halftone is to be shorter than the color shape.

These methods are used whether the art you are working with is a black and tone photograph or a black and tone illustration.

FIG. 63

If you use the overlay method, it can be prepared on the mechanical over the **photostat**.

You would use any of the methods shown in Fig. 62 **along with** the overlay. This assembly would leave little question as to what is required. The base mechanical is an indication for the black halftone only, and the overlay is specifically the shape for the second color.

An alternate method would be to prepare the overlay directly over the **original photograph**.

The choice will be determined by the type of job it is and the nature of the photo you are working with. If you are not certain which method to use, consult your production manager or printer.

FIG. 63

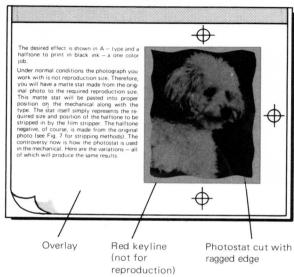

The desired effect is shown in A — type and a halftone to print in black ink — a one color job.

Under normal conditions the photograph you work with is not reproduction size. Therefore, you will have a matte stat made from the original photo to the required reproduction size. This matte stat will be pasted into proper position on the mechanical along with the type. The stat itself simply represents the required size and position of the halftone to be stripped in by the film stripper. The halftone negative, of course, is made from the original photo (see Fig. 7 for stripping methods). The controversy now is how the photostat is used in the mechanical. Here are the variations — all of which will produce the same results:

Overlay   Red keyline (not for reproduction)   Photostat cut with ragged edge

Methods B and/or D (Fig. 62), with or without the overlay, are the most acceptable approaches. However, be certain to indicate that the photostat is for size and position only — it is **not** "copy for camera." This is usually done by drawing a red or black "X" directly on the stat, and writing instructions either on the stat, in the margin or on a tissue over the stat. Simply write "Stat for size and position only. Strip in B/W HT from original art." An appropriate abbreviation for this is "FPO" (For Position only).

The overlay can be any of the types men-

FIG. 64

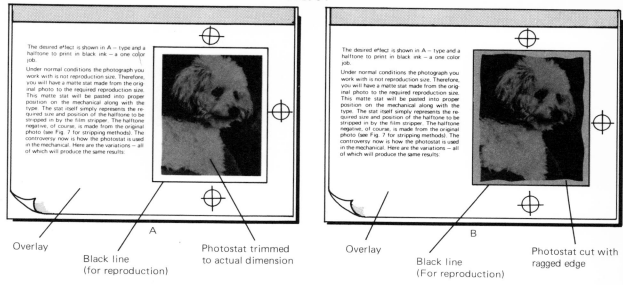

The desired effect is shown in A — type and a halftone to print in black ink — a one color job.

Under normal conditions the photograph you work with is not reproduction size. Therefore, you will have a matte stat made from the original photo to the required reproduction size. This matte stat will be pasted into proper position on the mechanical along with the type. The stat itself simply represents the required size and position of the halftone to be stripped in by the film stripper. The halftone negative, of course, is made from the original photo (see Fig. 7 for stripping methods). The controversy now is how the photostat is used in the mechanical. Here are the variations — all of which will produce the same results:

Overlay

Black line
(for reproduction)

A

Photostat trimmed
to actual dimension

The desired effect is shown in A — type and a halftone to print in black ink — a one color job.

Under normal conditions the photograph you work with is not reproduction size. Therefore, you will have a matte stat made from the original photo to the required reproduction size. This matte stat will be pasted into proper position on the mechanical along with the type. The stat itself simply represents the required size and position of the halftone to be stripped in by the film stripper. The halftone negative, of course, is made from the original photo (see Fig. 7 for stripping methods). The controversy now is how the photostat is used in the mechanical. Here are the variations — all of which will produce the same results:

Overlay

Black line
(For reproduction)

B

Photostat cut with
ragged edge

tioned in the previous chapters, i.e., black on acetate, amber film, etc. Place a tissue over the overlay and indicate the color that it represents. Incidentally, it is a good practice to write your specifications on the overlay itself as well as on the tissue. You can neatly place a piece of tape in the corner of the overlay and label it "solid blue" or "40% screen of red," etc.

FIG. 64

A common variation of this layout would be as shown in Fig. 64. The halftone area with color overprinting does not occupy the full dimension. It falls short of the overall size with a black rule framing it. In preparation the stat can be trimmed to the actual shape rather than a ragged edge and a black line ruled on the board. The overlay is cut to the same shape as the stat. A proper color break would leave little doubt as to the required results.

However, if the black line were to butt the halftone as in B, you would have to cut the stat with a ragged edge in order to preserve the black line.

115

PRESEPARATED TWO-COLOR TONE ART

FIG. 65

In Fig. 65 the base art (A) was done in line to hold detail in the black plate, while the black tone portions were rendered in grays on an overlay (B). The tone art for the second color was rendered in black and grays on a second overlay (C). A line negative of the base art was shot. Each tone overlay was then shot through a halftone screen at different angles to create two halftone negatives. Separate plates were made, the black line and halftone negatives combined into one plate, and the halftone negative of the second color produced the second plate. Each plate was then printed one over the other in its respective color.

While this use of two colors is simple, it is effective and relatively easy to control. If form, color and texture were critical, the art preparation would be more challenging.

Here we are concerned with **tone** separation. The platemaker will photoscreen the art — what you give him to work with is what you'll get — nothing more, perhaps less. He is not going to strip in tints and combinations. You must supply him with the proper tone values to create the color effects you have in mind.

Using this method, your selection of the proper quantities of black and white, representing the values of red, requires a good deal of ingenuity. For example, areas to be printed in full intensity of red will appear solid black on the overlay; lighter values will naturally be lighter values of gray

If you were to mix a 60% black (gray) and a 10% red, you would get a particular value of

black with a cast of red. Obviously, by changing the combination you would also change the color effect. If you were to mix the **two colors** directly, you would immediately see whether or not it is the value of color you desire and change it at will. But if you painted each color on a separate piece of paper, it would be quite difficult to **visualize** what they would look like if they were mixed. While this in itself is difficult, it becomes more complex when you substitute black for the red.

Now is the time to get to know your materials — especially paper. Until now we have only considered using acetate for overlays. There is no set rule as to the material you use for the overlay, as long as you can achieve the effect you want — and it can be photographed by the platemaker. Tonal values can be rendered on acetate, vellum, watercolor paper, frosted acetate — using paint, pencils, inks, markers — anything you need to produce the effect.

The strongest advice I can offer you at this time is to prepare a comprehensive color sketch of the exact results you hope to achieve before you start the finished art.

Only through experience, consultation with an excellent production manager or printer, and reference to screen color charts can successful results be obtained.

Unless the subject matter is simple, this method is not too popular among artists. What makes it difficult is the uncertainly of the results before printing.

Often it would be easier to prepare two-color process art or perhaps black tone art and shoot it as a duotone.

FIG. 65

A

Base art — black line to hold detail

B

Black tone areas rendered on overlay over base art

C

Red tone areas rendered in black and gray on second overlay

The red tone plate when printed by itself

Note: It is advisable to hinge each overlay along a different edge rather than build up excessive thickness with tapes placed over each other. Each overlay can then be lifted back and out of the way while working on the next one. This should also eliminate the refraction caused by two or more overlays.

Both plates when printed one over the other

117

FIG. 66

Black line art for black plate

PRESEPARATED TWO, THREE OR FOUR-COLOR TONE ART

This area of color separation could be classified as the most difficult of all hand separated techniques. To illustrate all the possibilities would, indeed, require many cumbersome volumes.

There are perhaps five aspects of tone separated art that are essential to its success:

One — illustration technique (or style). For the sake of simplification let us categorize this as realistic — slick or photographic, realistic — stylized, cartoon, or graphic design.

Two — a strong understanding of color. A sensitive, trained eye for discerning tonal values in both black and color. A vivid imagination in the use and interpretation of the printer's color chart.

Three — the stock upon which the art will be

Black tone art on overlay for the black plate

reproduced. It would be advisable to start a file of various stock samples and color combinations. These can be acquired by writing to various paper and ink manufacturers.

Four — you must have an unending knowledge of materials, tools, and drawing papers.

Five — a thorough knowledge and understanding of reproduction techniques.

Perhaps the most difficult of all types of illustration to preseparate is the realistic — photographic. One would have to possess a superior knowledge of, and experience with, the five afore-mentioned aspects. It is rarely, if ever, required — or successfully rendered. My advice would be to wait awhile before you attempt it professionally.

FIG. 66

Ordinarily, you will encounter the need for hand separated three and four-color tone art in book publishing — usually children's books, comic books, or low budget publications.

Black tone art on overlay for the blue plate

Black tone art on overlay for the yellow plate

Black tone art on overlay for the red plate

All four colors printed over each other

SELECTING COLORS

When printing in two (or more) colors, one color is usually black — to carry detail. If not black, a strong dark color is used.

Aside from the psychological and optical principles involved in color printing there are a number of significant variables. The nature of the tone art and the intensity of the second color is of course one of the principal considerations. If the tone art is dark and in low contrast, avoid printing a solid dark color over it. Chances are it will have poor readability and look muddy. Perhaps a screened tint of the color may be the solution. Tone art that is too light can be equally as troublesome as that which is too dark. Using a dark color over a light halftone might overpower it.

The paper's texture, color and ink absorption properties are major contributors to color variations. Usually the coated surfaces produce the more intense colors. Slight color deviations may be caused by the inks in conjunction with press variations, but can be controlled.

The kind of press used will also determine the color results. A color job run on a single-color press will produce decidedly different effects than if run on a four-color press or a two-color press.

Halftone screen size, the color combinations you choose and the sequence in which they are printed (called rotation) are also determining factors.

The color guide charts on the following pages are meant to act as an introduction to the enormity of the subject. They represent only a fraction of the color combinations that can be produced.

Realize as you study them that the same screens and ink printed on a different stock would produce different colors. There are probably thousands of different colored stocks — hundreds of shades of white alone — it staggers the imagination. The many paper and ink manufacturers have tons of literature, samples, color guides, etc., available at your request.

This is far from a subject you can just sit down and read about to develop expertise. You must see it, do it — live it. Attend trade shows and seminars, visit printers, photolabs and platemakers, write to manufacturers, collect samples and above all — ask questions.

Color Charts

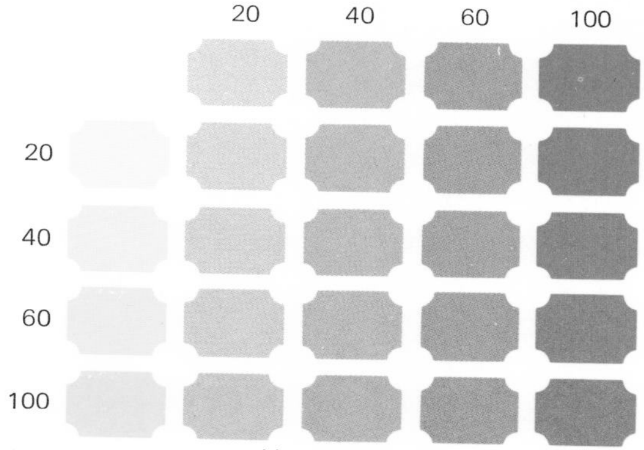

Yellow-Magenta

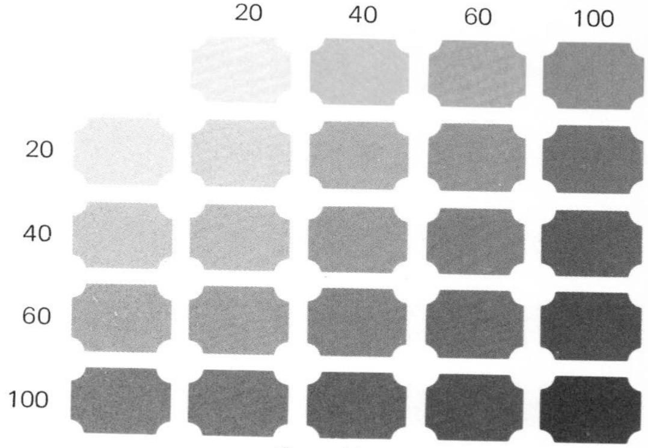

Cyan-Magenta

Yellow-Cyan

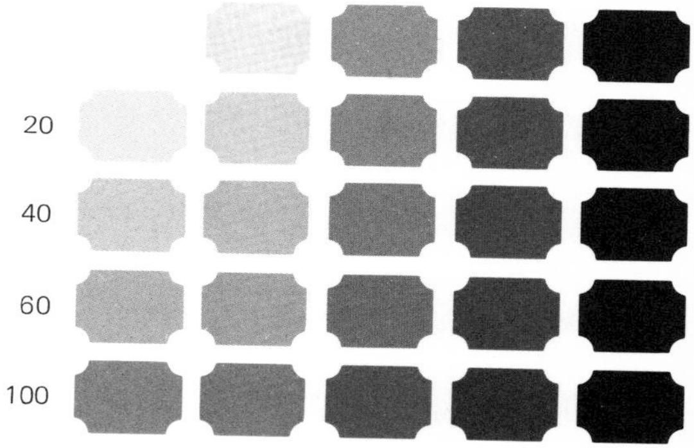

Cyan-Black

Yellow-Black

Magenta-Black

2 COLORS

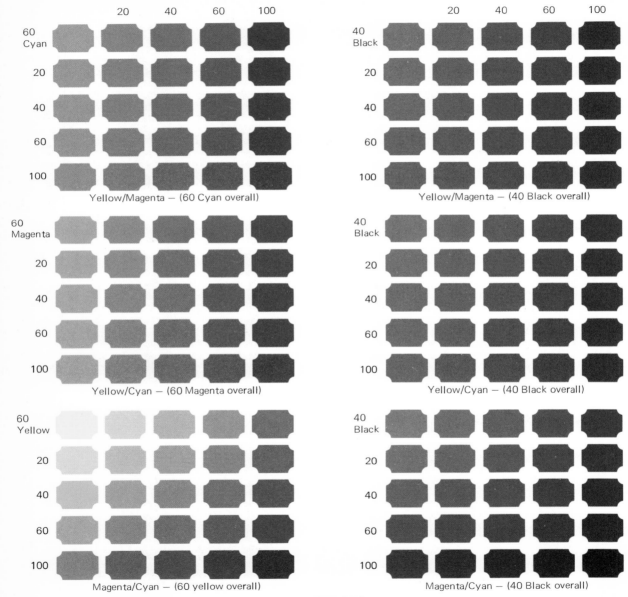

	20	40	60	100
60 Cyan				
20				
40				
60				
100				

Yellow/Magenta — (60 Cyan overall)

	20	40	60	100
40 Black				
20				
40				
60				
100				

Yellow/Magenta — (40 Black overall)

60 Magenta				
20				
40				
60				
100				

Yellow/Cyan — (60 Magenta overall)

40 Black				
20				
40				
60				
100				

Yellow/Cyan — (40 Black overall)

60 Yellow				
20				
40				
60				
100				

Magenta/Cyan — (60 yellow overall)

40 Black				
20				
40				
60				
100				

Magenta/Cyan — (40 Black overall)

3 COLORS

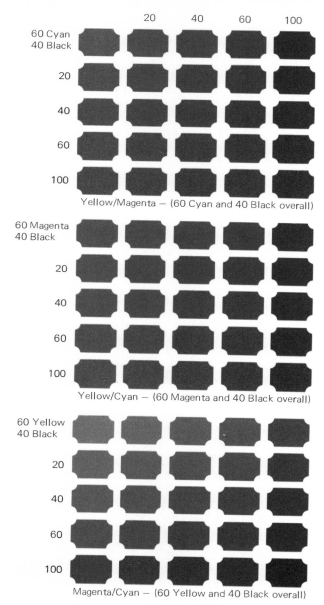

	20	40	60	100

60 Cyan
40 Black

20

40

60

100

Yellow/Magenta — (60 Cyan and 40 Black overall)

60 Magenta
40 Black

20

40

60

100

Yellow/Cyan — (60 Magenta and 40 Black overall)

60 Yellow
40 Black

20

40

60

100

Magenta/Cyan — (60 Yellow and 40 Black overall)

4 COLORS

If you have read this text thoroughly and do not have dozens of questions jetting through your mind — you had better go through it again. Because of the complexities and variables of the topics discussed you must realize that each is a subject within itself requiring further knowledge. Although you have come to the end of this book, it is not the end of the subject. Regard it as only the beginning. For as these pages are being written, someone, somewhere is compiling new facts and material that will add to the rapid development of reproduction methods. To comprehend further innovations, you must be familiar with the past and present. If you have studied this text carefully, you are off to a running start. I hope the gap between you and your goal has been made smaller.